Acknowledgments

When I was approached by Adams Media to write about parenting and talking to children, I was thrilled. After all, I am a parent, and I have made my living over the past decade sharing ideas about parenting. However, I had never presented my thoughts on parenting as flat-out advice. And as someone who would never presume to judge others (usually), it proved difficult to share my opinions. Luckily, Peter Archer and Ross Weisman at Adams Media were there to help me frame my experiences in a comfortable and informative manner, and I thank them for it. I only judged a little bit.

I would also like to thank my friend Mike Adamick, without whom I would have no coattails to ride upon. Nice coat, Mike.

Obviously, I could not write a book on communicating with kids if I did not have any. I am the father of two incredible, smart, sweet, and funny boys, Atticus and Zane, who have had the courtesy of putting me through many of the situations outlined in this book—the writing of which allowed me to rethink many of my previous actions and to learn from my own experiences. It's all so meta. I thank them for so much more than the words in this book.

My beautiful wife, Tricia, has been a fantastic partner in parenting from the beginning, and we have spent the past decade bouncing ideas off each other and trying to find which decisions stick. Some stick more than others. This book would never have come into being without her, and she deserves a byline more than an acknowledgment, but we'll keep it like this for tax reasons.

I would also like to thank my own parents, who have supplied years of inspiration (and continue to do so), and my sister, who has always been the bad one.

I'm kidding.

Contents

Introduction

You know that parent from the playground, the one who offers loud, unsolicited advice on your parenting options? That's not me. Sure, I take my kids to the playground, and I might chat people up a bit if there isn't any Wi-Fi, but I would never presume to tell them how to parent their child.

But isn't this a book on . . . ?

Yes. Yes, it is. This is, in fact, a book where I offer parenting advice. The difference is that you paid for this book, which makes my advice *solicited*. In fact, I'm a professional. That said, if you *didn't* pay for this book, then please tell your kid to quit throwing rocks; it's a playground not a quarry.

What Is a Phrase Book?

At this point you may be wondering, what exactly is a phrase book and what page is "quarry" on?

There are many kinds of phrase books, but for the most part they all perform the same sort of service: to bridge the gaps of language.

This particular book is designed to help parents better understand the situations that arise in the lives of their children and what phrases it is appropriate to use in resolving them. The book provides suggestions on what you should say, what you *shouldn't* say, and what may happen in each case.

It's kind of like that old TV show *Kids Say the Darndest Things*, with Art Linkletter and later Bill Cosby. But instead of famous, charming people laughing over school-kid semantics, you've got me yelling across the playground.

"Quarry" is on this page.

How to Use This Book

Now, when your kid presents you with a challenge—that is, throws a linguistic curveball—you've got a handy guide to refer to. No, this book does not double as a bat. Rather, it's a place for you to explore new angles, find common ground, and gain helpful insight into furthering meaningful conversation with your offspring, because there is nothing kids love more than meaningful conversation with their parents.

The trick is getting the same meaning from the same conversation. Or something close to it.

How do you use this phrase book? However you want, but what I suggest is reading it and then keeping it someplace handy to refer to as the situations I outline here actually arise. Many of them will, and then you can reap the benefits of my wisdom. Oh, the sweet, sweet wisdom.

Keep it in the bathroom. I'm okay with that.

One thing to bear in mind is that the phrases found in this book will be helpful only if you believe in them (apparently phrases are like fairies). Don't try to sell something that you wouldn't buy. Kids see right through that kind of thing. You know yourself, and you know your child—try to understand the given situation as best you can, and then use this book as a way to better the conversation, not end it.

Fine print: Obviously individual cases will vary. When in doubt, your best option is to follow your heart and do what you think is best for the specific child(ren) involved and the scenario at hand. You may not agree with what I offer, and that's fair. This is America, or some other country that sells my book, and discourse is healthy. The advice I offer is merely suggestion; granted, it is really awesome suggestion, but the words you use are entirely up to you. You are the parent; I'm just some guy on the playground.

Now go forth and talk to your kids. And remember, it starts with a listen.

PART I
Life Lessons

CHAPTER 1

Discipline: Enforcing Rules and Pushing Limits

A great deal has been published about how to discipline children appropriately—about whether it's through punishment or training. Those books, for the most part, are written by people with a lot of letters after their name and a framed piece of paper declaring them experts on the matter. However, none of that guarantees that they have any actual experience with children of their own. Fortunately, I have plenty.

My children enjoy a good limit pushing, and I enjoy quashing such things like so many broken hopes and dreams.

Actually, I am a fan of children testing their limits; after all, do we want our children to rise to the status quo, or to look for ways to go beyond it? The latter requires thinking outside the box, and that box tends to be sealed shut with the lacquer of implied limitations.

It is up to us, as parents and caregivers, to discern the reasoning behind our disciplinary reactions. Are the kids actually doing something wrong that might harm them or others, or do their actions simply defy the default setting of *just the way it is*?

Obviously, there are plenty of times when a child's actions (or lack thereof) require consequences based on established rules and a clear understanding of them. That's good. Those moments teach responsibility (among other lessons), and it is important for parents to enforce such things, but it is also beneficial to allow some wiggle room in defining the limits of what we are willing to accept.

In this chapter we'll look at situations where a child has indeed run afoul of clear and reasonable rules of behavior. This does not mean that I think your kid is going to do bad things. Your kid is an angel. I'm just worried about the rest of the people reading this book.

Also, by starting with worst-case scenarios, we are saving tons of pages of backstory and getting right into the conversations that are likely to follow.

It's for the environment. You're welcome.

It Wasn't Me, and Other Rivers in Egypt

Denial is the classic go-to response for many children (and adults) when confronted with an accusation of wrongdoing. For example, consider the popular comic strip *The Family Circus* by the late Bil Keane, now drawn by his son Jeff Keane. Those kids are haunted by the gremlins Not Me and Nobody, and they never admit to squat. Chances are your family has similar gremlins running around your home. Don't feed them after midnight!

TYPICAL PHRASE YOU MAY HEAR: *It wasn't me!*

VARIATIONS: *I didn't do it. Someone else did it. I don't know what happened.*

This phrase, usually delivered with an amazing flair for the dramatic that borders on Oscar consideration, can mean one of two things: Either the child is innocent, or he is responsible for the misdeed and is trying to get away with it.

In this scenario we're going to assume the child has broken a rule. The question becomes, why is he trying to get away with it? Is he afraid of the punishment such behavior warrants, or is he ashamed of disappointing us? Or both?

Both motivations are legit. While recognizing that, you should also recognize that this is a great opportunity to explain why the child's actions result in such feelings.

Experiencing shame upon disappointing you is evidence, on one level, that you've done a good parenting job. Your child doesn't want to let you down; he doesn't want to provoke a negative emotion from you.

On the other hand, fearing punishment and trying to avoid it are basic survival instincts. This is where you can explain to your offspring that accepting responsibility is a bigger boon to his character than denying it. You can also remind him that the long-term benefits of doing the right thing, rather than holding onto a belly full of guilt, are worth a few brief moments of discomfort.

Before you have that discussion, though, you've got to solve the conundrum with which your kid has confronted you: Who's really responsible for the misdeed? At last that box set of *Murder, She Wrote* is finally going to pay for itself. It is time to solve a mystery, parents!

WHAT TO SAY: *If you didn't do it, then who did?*

At this point any other children and/or pets in the vicinity should (a) begin brushing up on their own alibis, and (b) start looking for a potential exit from the area. The child in question will either finally admit guilt or pass the buck, since he knows full well that somebody is going down.

Of course, the newly blamed party might actually *be* guilty (or the denial train adds another car and just keeps chugging), and you should address that accordingly, but let's assume that you've already identified the culprit (though you haven't told him so). Now we'll focus on the clues and consequences of such blame-shifting behavior.

FOLLOW-UP: *Do you think (named party) should be punished for something that you did?*

Feel free to go deeper into "Two wrongs don't make a right" territory on this one. At some point the child will, you hope, come clean, and a punishment befitting the crime, with added consideration for obstruction of justice, can be handed down.

WHAT NOT TO SAY: *I know it was you. You broke my heart.*

Aside from the impulse to quote *The Godfather II* or sing fairly inappropriate Shaggy lyrics, the main thing to avoid is jumping straight into anger-filled accusations. There are a number of natural responses to "It wasn't me." and you could easily deliver any one of them with the raised voice and intimidating tension that drive the truth even further away. Keep your anger in check (I know, easier said than done) and put the responsibility—and the opportunity—for doing the right thing squarely on the child's small, suddenly cornered shoulders. He might surprise you. Eventually.

What's in a Blame?

Some kids might have more trouble learning the "Don't blame" lesson than others (where "others" equals those kids wrongly accused). Here are two steps you should try to avoid:

1. Believe the blamer (but not really). If the child insists on blaming another despite absolute proof of his guilt, some parents, as a ruse, blame the other, too. They hope that letting the blamer see an innocent person punished will cause some decency to kick in. The problem, of course, is what to do if the first child says nothing. Since you can't reasonably punish the innocent child, sooner or later you'll have to own up to the deception.

2. Give the child a taste of his own medicine. This is also a ruse. Some parents will ask another child to blame the blamer for something he didn't do and then take disciplinary action as if he had done it. "Let him see how *he* likes it" is the logic here. But all this is really teaching the child is to become a more effective liar.

THE SECOND ONE ALWAYS GETS CAUGHT

Phrases like *he started it* and *she hit me first* are incredibly common (we'll talk more about the concept of "first" later in this book). In each case the child making the claim may be telling the truth, but it's a tough call. This used to be a big problem in the National Football League, where the player retaliating for a foul was often the one caught and penalized—but the NFL now has the ability to review the film. As a parent, you don't (usually) have this ability. Instead, this becomes a perfect opportunity to encourage kids to work out their own differences. Something along the lines of, "Since we can't agree on what happened, I can either punish both of you, or you can work together to figure out a better solution" usually gets the ball rolling.

The Fine Line Between Tattling and Telling

Nobody likes a tattletale. This is widely accepted as social fact. Yet we, the adults, are constantly reminding our children that they need to tell us, the parents, teachers, and assorted other authority figures, when someone is misbehaving. So which is it: to tell or not to tell? That is the question.

TYPICAL PHRASE YOU MAY HEAR: *Jimmy did _____!*

First, Jimmy didn't really do anything. I made him up. I don't want any letters from Jimmy, his friends, his family, or other concerned citizens. Relax, Jimmy.

To the point, why does the child telling on Jimmy feel obligated to do so, and is the telling justified?

It depends heavily on what it is that Jimmy is doing. If he is throwing rocks at kids on the playground, that makes his actions dangerous, and he should be reported. If he is picking his nose, then he's just lacking in social graces and should wash his hands.

Fine lines can be confusing.

Kids tell for many reasons. They may be wanting for attention, deflecting their own negative behavior, or feeling honorbound by the deep threads of justice. It could be a good deed or downright annoying, and you, as parents, can only address each instance as it comes along and take the opportunity to explain why that particular piece of information belongs in one pile or the other.

Example One

Your child tells on Jimmy because he is throwing rocks at the other kids on the playground. Let's assume that no one, at this point, has been hurt.

WHAT TO SAY: *Thank you for telling me.*

First, speak to Jimmy or the person watching him to ensure that he stops. This is important, because you don't want anyone to be hurt. Next, seize the opportunity to work on the subtle distinctions among different kinds of telling. Ask the child if she knows *why* it was important that she tell an adult what Jimmy was doing. Emphasize that Jimmy's behavior was dangerous and that, by letting you know about it, she was able to protect others. This is the kind of telling we need more of. Maybe throw out the word "hero." Kids love that.

WHAT NOT TO SAY: *Go tell him to stop.*

Your kid just got hit with a rock.

VARIATIONS: *I don't care. It's none of your business what he's doing.*

Now more kids are down with rock injuries.

Example Two

Your child tells on Jimmy because he is picking his nose.

WHAT TO SAY: *That's pretty gross, but it's his nose.*

VARIATIONS: *He's not hurting anyone else, even though it's nasty. We'll let his parents take care of it.*

Stating that nose picking is gross or nasty is a great way to reinforce personal hygiene and social courtesies with your child, which is a bonus. Declaring that the nose in question belongs to Jimmy implies that he has a personal space, as we all do, and that we should respect that. It would be perfectly acceptable if your child wanted to tell Jimmy that picking his nose in public is gross (without going so far as to tease him), because there is always the chance that he didn't realize it. Jimmy's just a kid.

WHAT NOT TO SAY: *Nobody likes a tattletale.*

I know, I opened with that quip, and most of us agree that it is true, but I am a professional. Don't try it at home.

A child who is told, "Nobody likes a tattletale," with the unspoken implication that *she* is a tattletale, can quickly lose sight of the lesson being taught and find herself overcome with embarrassment, sadness, and insecurity—none of which furthers the discussion at hand. These feelings do, however, prompt tears, and nobody likes a crybaby. Making tattling the focus of the discussion also means that in the future, when the child sees something important and potentially dangerous—like Jimmy throwing rocks at somebody—she'll recall your words, and she won't tell anybody.

Tattle and Telling: The Blame Brothers

John's older son entered the living room at a run. "Dad!" he yelled. "Tim's throwing shoes at me!"

John sighed internally and followed Robert down the hall to the bedroom the boys shared. A shoe shot through the open door. It would have hit John had he not stopped mid-stride. Instead it banged off the wall and fell on the floor. The boy who threw it followed his shot with another shoe, hurling the second one quick and true. It found its target in Robert's stomach. "See?" Robert howled.

"Tattletale!" came Tim's voice from behind the bed.

"Tim," John said sharply. "Come out from there. I want to talk to you."

The younger boy emerged, a shoe still in one hand. John sat down on the bed. "Put that down, please," he told Tim.

"He's a *tattletale*!" snapped Tim at his brother.

"No," John said calmly. "What you were doing was dangerous." He turned to Robert. "Thank you for telling me." Now he turned back to Tim. "Tim, throwing anything at anybody is dangerous, and it isn't the way to solve a problem. Why were you doing it?"

Tim shuffled his feet and glared at Robert. "He was making fun of me. And he picks his nose!"

"Who's a tattletale now?" snapped Robert.

"Robert, be quiet please," John told him. He turned back to the younger boy. "It was wrong of Robert to make fun of you, and he'll apologize in a minute, but it was very wrong of you to throw things. If Robert picks his nose, it's unsanitary, and I hope he stops, but that's nothing for you to be concerned about."

He rose, facing Robert. "Robert, were you making fun of your brother? If you were, then please apologize." Robert muttered something that might have been "Sorry."

"Thank you." John put a hand on the boy's shoulder. "Now let's talk about nasal hygiene."

Welcome to parenting.

Adorable Little Liars

You may have noticed a recurring theme in the previous two entries, and it will continue to play a part in the discussion that follows, because, frankly, kids love it. I'm speaking, of course, about lying.

There are many different types of lies, from little white fibs to great big whoppers, and many of us still use them to varying degrees in our adult life—certainly it is better to stick to the former.

It isn't that kids are more devious than adults. Rather, the concept of lying is new to them, and they have to establish the boundaries of it. You can help with that.

There are lies of malice and deceit, but most of the lies that children tell fall into the category of hyperbole—tall tales. Children often put creative spins on their own reality in hopes of impressing others, avoiding punishment, or amusing themselves.

It is up to parents to help children recognize the difference between the stretched truths of humorous imagination and the kinds of falsehoods that can result in real and serious consequences.

Obviously, nobody wants his or her child to become a pathological liar, but the other side of the coin is that, according to the Internet, young children with a penchant for inventive fabrication and exaggerated storytelling tend to score higher than others on IQ tests. It was on the Internet, so it must be true.

Example One

TYPICAL PHRASE YOU MAY HEAR: *The dog ate my homework.*

I'm a sucker for the classics.

There are many factors at play as you're formulating the proper response to this kind of lie. The important thing is that you need to determine the child's intent in presenting it and to consider the ramifications it may have for the situation at hand. For instance, were you and your child talking in a humorous (or at least somewhat humorous) mood, or did the lie come in response to a serious request for an honest statement?

WHAT TO SAY: *(The choice here is to either play along or cut it short.)*

(PLAYING ALONG) *Then you need to follow the dog around until it poops your homework out—and your teacher isn't going to be happy about it.*

(CUTTING IT SHORT) *Either you are making up a story, in which case you need to do your homework right now, or the dog has a serious problem and we will get rid of it. Which choice do you want to make?*

One thing to keep in mind is that the child usually offers this sort of lie when he's fully aware that you will not believe it, so the lie is not an attempt to pull a fast one. He simply hopes to turn the conversation in a new direction, away from a topic that may be causing him stress or embarrassment. For example, he may not have his homework because he had trouble comprehending the subject matter. Maybe there are other extenuating circumstances beyond his control. Or maybe he just likes getting a laugh. Who doesn't need one of those?

Example Two

The child is telling you a lie with the intent to purposefully deceive or mislead for nefarious reasons. This isn't to say the child is some sort of diabolical super-villain in training, but it does suggest that he hasn't considered any consequences other than the one benefitting himself. Shocking, isn't it?

TYPICAL PHRASE YOU MAY HEAR: *Timmy fell in the well!*

WHAT TO SAY: *I'll call the police!*

VARIATION: *I'll call his parents.*

The answer here is even more delicate than in Example One because you may need to err on the side of caution and treat the situation with the appropriate seriousness that it requires Did the lying result in serious actions that would not have been taken had the truth been told? Was anyone injured? A lie of this caliber is not a creative outlet but a clear disregard for rules, safety, and the feelings of others. You should implement a fair and clear punishment in line with the severity of the situation.

LYING AS A SYMPTOM

Lying, generally speaking, is not a cause for alarm, but in some cases lies may be a symptom of more serious issues. Often children who are victims (or perpetrators) of abuse, bullying, or other significant behavior will lie out of embarrassment, fear, shame, or lack of understanding. If you suspect that a child is using lies to hide matters of a serious and dangerous nature, please contact the appropriate authorities.

Under Peer Pressure

Hypothetically speaking, if everyone was jumping off a cliff, would you do it too? The answer you want to hear, of course, is a remorseful "No." This question, after all, was created to make a point, and it's been driving that point home for generations. Just because everyone else is doing something doesn't mean *you* have to do it. It is okay to make your own decisions and do what you feel is right, regardless of the mob mentality and the gleam of freshly polished pitchforks. Think for yourself.

But what do we know about the cliff? Is it a great drop to certain death? Or is it the platform from which endless summer cannonballs have been launched into crystal pools of clear mountain water?

The point is that thinking for yourself is generally the right thing to do, but don't rule out the possibility of the child considering carefully and then choosing to jump off the cliff on pure principle. Thinking for oneself means considering all the options, even those chosen by the masses.

And some situations do indeed arise in which the right thing to do, metaphorically speaking, is *always* to step away from the cliff. That said, it's still a good idea to reinforce the idea that your child has a choice.

TYPICAL PHRASE YOU MAY HEAR: *But everybody else is doing it!*

The cliff is not the issue. Most likely the child does not have a deep, inner need to jump off a steep piece of rock but, rather, an overwhelming desire to belong. It doesn't matter what everybody else is doing; what matters is that they are doing *something*, and your child doesn't want to be left out.

WHAT TO SAY: *Why do you want to do it?*

VARIATIONS: *Why is everyone else doing it? Would you want to do it if they weren't?*

The goal here is not to talk the child out of doing something (unless that something actually involves a cliff), but to encourage her to examine the reason(s) why she wants to do it, weigh the consequences, and make a well-thought-out decision.

WHAT NOT TO SAY: *I don't care what everyone else is doing.*

VARIATION: *I'm not the boss of everybody; I'm the boss of you.*

Remember, this isn't about saying no to one particular event. Rather, you're trying to instill in the child the understanding that participating in this and all future actions should be carefully considered prior to engagement. The fact is that children will face countless situations like this over the years, and most of them will occur when you're not around—often when *no* adults are around. Our highest goal as parents is not to make well-reasoned decisions for our kids, but to empower them to decide for themselves.

SHAMING INTO ACTION

Some of the biggest issues that children face in terms of peer pressure, such as drug use and sexual activity, arise in situations that are likely to occur at ages far younger than anyone will ever be comfortable with. By empowering children with the confidence to say no to peer pressure, you aren't just giving them the tools for strength in character; you're also providing an important weapon that will ensure their own survival.

There will be numerous times when kids must stand up to would-be negative influencers, armed only with what we have given them. They will face that common device of mob mentality: the "calling out" or public shaming of those reluctant to join. The idea behind such tactics is to make kids feel small, uncool, or unimportant if they do not take part in the group experience. Children need to know that there are other options—and that they are strong enough to choose them.

Crime and Punishment

Retributive justice states that the punishment should fit the crime. That sounds reasonable, but more important, it reminds us that there's a difference between retribution and vengeance. The purpose of punishment is not to "get even" but to hold the offender accountable. Punishment should be firm, fair, and lacking in any sort of revenge or spite. Remember, we are trying to mold better citizens, not break their spirit.

Although parenting styles may vary, it is also important to consider that each child will respond differently to various forms of punishment. One child might see the error of his ways when he loses privileges. Another might get it after you give him a stern talking to—the secret is finding what works best for the individual and adapting the appropriate level to support the lesson you are hoping to teach.

TYPICAL PHRASE YOU MAY HEAR: *That's not fair!*

VARIATIONS: *I shouldn't be grounded. I don't want to lose any privileges!*

Nobody likes to be reprimanded or punished, even when she knows she deserves it. However, consequences are not supposed to be fun, and taking responsibility for one's inappropriate actions and making amends is not intended to be easy. The key is to make the child understand that the punishment is in line with her own actions. There is nothing wrong with letting her be active in the sentencing process.

WHAT TO SAY: *What do you think is fair?*

VARIATION: *It is fair (and explain why).*

This is a great opportunity for the child to give deep thought to her misdeed and to develop some empathy about the ramifications of it. It is not an opportunity for her to suggest a trip to the candy store as appropriate justice. Give her clear options and let her counter.

In an ideal scenario, you'll see a moment of clarity within the child in which she comes to terms with both her wrongdoing and the disciplinary action that resulted.

Unfortunately, in some cases that just doesn't happen. In such cases, the original punishment (or some variation of it) should be imposed, but at least the child knows the action is based on reason—even if she doesn't like it.

WHAT NOT TO SAY: *If you can't do the time, don't do the crime.*

VARIATION: *You shouldn't have been caught.*

Such remarks might seem harmless, but in reality they offer the determined child an out that may lead to further bad behavior. Essentially, you're saying that sneakier and more elaborate schemes will be rewarded. This avoids the reconciliation that comes from the child understanding what she did wrong and taking responsibility for her actions.

We want our children to learn lessons from their lapses in judgment, not to try harder to "get away with it."

On paper, a fair justice system works wonders.

A CASE AGAINST SPANKING

Spanking used to be the default setting for many parents. It was simple, it was quick, and it left no doubt that an offense was committed. But even though spanking is painful, it hasn't always proved to be very effective. Sure, a child who fears the paddle might let that fear keep him from repeating the misdeed, but that is not a lesson, that is just conditioning. The child is basing his decision on fear, not on the understanding that other forms of punishment are more likely to provide.

The popular argument for spanking, *Spare the rod and spoil the child*, is true only for parents who lack imagination. There are many ways to discipline a child without causing him pain—ways that instill in him a clearer distinction between right and wrong, while maintaining the bond of trust he has with you to protect him from harm, not inflict it on him.

Young and Old Yeller

Yelling, as a form of communication, is all the rage these days. It's like texting, but less work for your thumbs. Nobody wants to walk downstairs, outside, or around the corner to speak to someone—why bother when a yell can deliver the message so much more easily? After all, the sofa is really comfortable, and the acoustics in the house are very impressive.

There's a difference, of course, between yelling *to* and yelling *at*. Yelling *to* is conveying a normal message in a louder tone in order to cover other noises and/or distance. Yelling *at* is generally done in moments of heightened emotion, and it is rarely good.

Therefore, the main problem with yelling lies in its context. When yelling as an act of anger becomes a tool for discipline, it is hard for children to tell where one ends and one begins. Even though anger in any situation that requires disciplinary action is generally unavoidable, your punishment should not be fueled by that anger.

Yelling only compounds the matter, and it cuts both ways. Kids can yell, too.

TYPICAL PHRASE YOU MAY HEAR: *I hate you!*

VARIATIONS: *Leave me alone! I never want to speak to you again! I never want to see you again!*

These are the kinds of outbursts that break a parent's heart. Obviously, despite any heat of the moment, you never want to hear the most important person in your life yell such awful things. After all, once they are said, they are said, and regardless of the apologies and forgiveness that follow, those words can never be un-heard.

WHAT TO SAY: *I understand that you are angry. Gather yourself and let's talk about it.*

VARIATIONS: *Take a moment. Count to ten.*

It is, understandably, hard to remain calm and collected when someone is yelling at you. When that someone is your child saying hurtful things, it is all the harder.

There are a number of ways to react, and they depend primarily on the issue(s) at hand and the general disposition of the angry party.

The child may be able to calm down with a few short breaths, or he may need to take a walk and a bit more time. Your job as a parent is to ensure that both he and you take the proper steps, and then get to the bottom of the matter in a more civilized fashion.

WHAT NOT TO SAY: *I hate you, too!*

Speaking these words will haunt you forever. Most people would agree that they shouldn't be used in any situation, but anger brings out the ugliness and lets it run corrosively amok. Don't let an angry moment lead to years of regret. Take your own advice about cooling down, and proceed in a manner that won't strain the most important relationship that a parent can have.

Bedtime Blues

Bedtime can be a wonderful moment between child and parent, when the tiredness of the day is tucked into deep slumber by sweet stories and soft whispers. Or it can be a living nightmare of stubborn refusal and endless frustration. I've seen it both ways.

Clearly, there are serious and practical reasons why children need to get plenty of sleep, most of them related to the children's continued health (a case can be made for safeguarding the health of the parent as well). But how firmly we hold the line on bedtime is an entirely personal matter. Some parents establish a rigid schedule to which the child must adhere no matter what. Other parents are incredibly flexible. As long as the child is getting enough sleep and is alert in school, it doesn't really matter when he sleeps (except to those who disagree with your choice). Every home is different.

TYPICAL PHRASE YOU MAY HEAR: *I'm not tired.*

VARIATIONS: *I don't want to go to bed. I want to stay up.*

Of course they do. The worry that most kids have is that by going to bed, they are going to miss something *awesome*. Our job is to convince them otherwise.

WHAT TO SAY: *You need to go to sleep. You aren't missing anything.*

VARIATIONS: *You need a good night of rest. Sleep is important!*

Depending on the child, you may be able to reason with him about why sleep is essential, but it is more likely that you will have to stand firm and feel like a jerk. Remember, it is literally for his own good.

Don't be afraid to have some fun with it.

VARIATIONS: *You can stay up, but . . .*

- You'll have to clean the toilets with your toothbrush.
- You'll have to write a ten-page paper on why you aren't going to bed.
- You'll have to do jumping jacks the whole time.

The idea is to create an alternative that makes bed look like the better choice. Seriously, who wants to do jumping jacks for an hour? Even kids who know you are joking will generally go along with it.

WHAT NOT TO SAY: *Get your butt in bed!*

VARIATION: *If you don't go to bed, you're grounded.*

With each subsequent excuse the child makes to get out of bed ("I have to go to the bathroom again"; "I need a drink of water"; "There are monsters under the bed") it is easy for parents to grow increasingly frustrated. Don't let the sleep-deprived tots push your buttons! Remember, bed is not a punishment, it is a necessity. Kids may not understand how important it is, but adults do. Keep in mind that firmness and anger are not the same thing.

Besides, there are worse ways for you to spend your time than reading one extra book or receiving one more kiss.

These are the problems we will one day miss.

The Other Side of Lullabies

It is late. The hallway is empty save the echoes of wonder—it is joy and they do not care who knows it. Their imagination is held within four walls and falling shades of darkness, but it sparkles in laughter and rolls forever, boundless. They are down the hall from me, and they are a world away. I am in the living room, content and fat and lazy.

Bedtime is a gamble. It is a spin of the wheel, a ball bouncing over colors, numbers, fading memories of days we have almost forgotten, and so many hopes of days ahead. It flirts with sudden snores and cries for cups of water. It skips across stories told, dreams unfolding, and sweet kisses that wish goodnight. We make our bets, never knowing where the ball will stop; all we know is that its final resting place will be a surprise.

Tonight it landed long after my footsteps faded, and they let their whispered words inspire them to action—quiet conversations built upon a rising crescendo until those once tucked in became undone, and the only things covered were sheets by shadows and the soft undersides of bouncing feet.

"But we're not tired," they say, and I tell them that they are.

"We don't want to miss anything!" they shout between the complaints of springs.

"You aren't missing anything," I answer.

"Yes we are, Daddy. We are missing this!" and their laughter is something I cannot argue with.

I stand in the doorway with the night behind me and a book in hand. Their eyes are bright and turned upward at the corners.

"Will you read us one last story?" asks one boy.

"We promise to go to bed when you are done," adds the other.

And so I turn some pages until all that is left is silent moonlight and the lingering sound of memories. I kiss them for good measure.

Catching Flies

There is a popular saying that you can catch more flies with honey than with vinegar. Of course, this leads one to ask why you would want to catch flies at all, but more important, what does the old saw actually *mean*?

It means that we are much more likely to achieve the results we want by being kind than by being mean. It makes a lot of sense, and most of us try to heed that advice in our lives. However, it is especially helpful in the realm of child–parent relations.

In theory, kindness begets kindness, so this is one of the most natural and beneficial choices we can make as parents.

Let us assume, as unlikely as it may sound, that you have asked a child to do something she isn't entirely thrilled about.

TYPICAL PHRASE YOU MAY HEAR: *I don't want to!*

VARIATION: *You can't make me!*

Despite her refusal to do said something, you are resolved to see it done (by her), and things could get ugly. This is your "honey or vinegar" moment.

WHAT TO SAY: *Look, I understand that you don't want to do it, but it is something that you need to do. Do this, and then you can do something that you want to do.*

VARIATIONS: *This is your responsibility. This is your contribution to the project. The faster you start, the sooner you will be done.*

Honey—as opposed to vinegar—is not about bribes or compromise. Don't promise treats or something special to make the child do what is expected of her. Honey is about treating the child with respect and providing explanations and reasons as needed. There can be positive results on the other side of the task at hand, but they should be legitimately connected to it or to its completion, not manufactured to bend the child to your will. Bribes are the beginning of a downward spiral, and those seldom end well for anyone.

WHAT NOT TO SAY: *You will do what I tell you.*

VARIATIONS: *I'm the boss. Just do it.*

Granted, the honey option may, should the child remain uncooperative, transition toward vinegar territory, but there is no reason to *start* there. The heavy-handed *because I'm your parent* act is where kids build resentment. Although they may toe the line a bit quicker in this environment, they are doing so out of fear, not because of the respect that such actions are presumably designed to call upon.

Kindness and reasonableness are much more likely to foster a growing sense of pride in accomplishment and responsibility. These are the lessons that last a lifetime.

CHAPTER 2

Apathy versus Empathy: Self-Confidence and Doing the Right Thing

Each generation accuses the subsequent ones of apathy, even though that sweeping generalization doesn't always hold true. Children are naturally empathic, but society likes to wring it out of them through the numbness-inducing twenty-four-hour news cycle, a general disregard for the effects of glorified violence in the movies and video games and on television, and a persistent focus on the problems of the individual at the expense of the problems of the population at large. If older generations believe the youth of today are apathetic, they have no one to blame but themselves.

The best way to teach kids to embrace their empathy and try to make a difference in their community (and thereby, in the world) is by showing them. If we, the parents, are active in doing the right thing, then our children will see the benefits of our actions and want to add their efforts to ours.

Those benefits don't extend just to those directly affected by our actions. The best part of doing good is that you reap many rewards yourself. There is no better way to help children feel better about themselves than encouraging them to help others. This chapter is about allowing kids to care and encouraging them to do the right thing.

Helping Others

All over the world, there are people suffering from illness, natural disasters, war, and hate—they are on television and the Internet every night, and their plight tugs at our heartstrings (and rightly so). But what about those we walk by every day? There are people starving on the corner. Someone down the street is sad and lonely. One of the kids in your child's class doesn't have a coat, and winter is coming. People need help, and when we are able to give it, we should do so. It is the right thing to do.

TYPICAL PHRASE YOU MAY HEAR: *Why is that person asking for money?*

VARIATION: *Why do we have to donate toys, food, and clothes?*

The answers don't have to be tough. Keep your explanations simple, and adjust them according to your child's age, maturity level, and depth of concern. There are a number of ways to discuss the troubles that people face. The key is in setting the tone. Speak of others with kindness. The truth is easy and clear:

Teach children to treat everyone with respect, and they will do it—respecting you, and themselves, in the process.

WHAT TO SAY: *That person is asking for money because, for reasons we don't know, she doesn't have any. She needs money to eat.*

VARIATION: *We donate toys, food, and clothes because there are people who don't have any of those things, and those are items nobody should go without.*

This advice may rub some of you the wrong way. You're teaching your kids about the entitled masses looking for handouts; you don't believe in encouraging such interactions of goodwill.

All I can say to you is that at the end of the day, helping others is the right thing to do. Children who understand that will always be the better for it. We all will.

WHAT NOT TO SAY: *That person is lazy and just wants a handout.*

VARIATION: *What those people need is a job.*

Passing judgment on other people is a terrible, ugly habit, and passing it along to our children is not doing them any favors. Obviously, there are those who abuse the kindness of others, but we shouldn't let the misdeeds of the few increase the suffering of the many. Frankly, many of those less fortunate would probably appreciate a job if it were available. However, it is impossible to know why some people need our help more than others until we take a walk in their shoes. They have enough problems, and it is not our place to add to them.

Teaching children to ignore the suffering of others is to rob them of their compassion, and that is a terrible injustice.

The Selfish Child

Although children tend by nature to be empathic, a strong case can also be made that they are innately selfish. They're complicated. Most kids are not selfish by the standard definition of the word. Rather, what we perceive as their selfishness is a complex blend of innocence and ignorance.

Children often experience a multitude of new things at once—the type of stuff that the rest of us seldom stop to acknowledge anymore. For example, their first time in a city might include their first subway and cab rides, their first live show in a theater, and the first time they have walked in public areas that smell of urine. It is a lot to take in and we've seen it. But it is new to them, and from their point of view, if they haven't seen it before, then nobody else has either.

Basically, a child has no reason to believe that the world does not revolve around her. That's kind of cute (for a while).

TYPICAL PHRASE YOU MAY HEAR: *It's mine. I found it.*

VARIATION: *That rainbow is for me.*

The "it" in the first phrase could be anything, from a discarded penny to the Grand Canyon. There is no filter of perspective here—like Neil Armstrong before them, they are finding things we all can see and claiming them. (At least Armstrong claimed the moon for all mankind, so that's not quite as selfish.)

WHAT TO SAY: *Nobody can own the Grand Canyon; it belongs to the earth, and to a lesser extent to the National Park Service.*

VARIATION: *Yes, that rainbow is for you. I made a call.*

It may seem like a simple thing, but explaining to children that some things are there for everyone to enjoy—that is, the child isn't the only one who matters—is actually great groundwork for more personal conversations and situations down the road.

As for the rainbow, give it with a wink and take these moments whenever you can.

WHAT NOT TO SAY: *You can have anything you want.*

VARIATION: *Whatever you want, I will buy it for you.*

This may seem sweet when the children are young, but it won't be long before you find yourself having to explain that some things cannot be bought or owned. This in turn gives the child reason to doubt the reliability of your promises.

Clearly, nothing good can come from buying a child whatever she wants.

Children who believe all problems can be solved with money grow up into adults who think all problems can be solved with money. They can't, and even those that can are often solved at prices far too high.

Giving and Receiving

At the most basic level, giving and receiving are really about sharing. Sharing is a big part of life, and coming to terms with it as a child can be frustrating, confusing, and—when it clicks—absolutely wonderful.

There is a reason why the old adage "It is better to give than to receive" has lasted all these years: It's true.

But receiving is pretty awesome, too.

The easy example here is Christmas or Hanukkah, the season when giving and receiving often happen at the same time. However, the principle also applies to birthdays and other occasions; feel free to substitute the gift-swapping occasion of your choice.

TYPICAL PHRASE YOU MAY HEAR: *I want this for Christmas.*

VARIATIONS: *I want that for Hanukkah. Are you going to get me these for Christmas?*

Did you spot the pattern? Kids love the idea of getting gifts. Luckily, they are pretty happy about giving, too.

WHAT TO SAY: *Why do you want that?*

VARIATION: *Why is that a good gift?*

The idea here to get the kid to think about why she actually wants something—not just because it is shiny and all the other kids have one, but why she *really* thinks that it is the right gift for her. Let her know that, yes, she will receive gifts for the holiday, but she should understand that presents are expensive, and she should ask only for things she really wants. Even Santa is on a budget.

Letting the child consider the how and why of gifts makes her a better giver, too. Once she starts thinking about which gift is best and why, she'll put similar thought into the presents she picks for others.

WHAT NOT TO SAY: *You better be good.*

VARIATION: *You need to act nicer if you want something for Hanukkah.*

By telling kids to be good—which is hard to avoid, thanks to every holiday special and song suggesting its importance—we are proclaiming that gifts are something earned. Hence the child's behavior is to be held in check by the promise of potential reward.

However, the idea behind giving and receiving gifts, whether they be wrapped in ribbons and bows, delivered hot from the oven, or offered to mark occasions like birthdays, graduations, weddings, retirements, and thank yous, is that *they are given from the heart*. They express your appreciation of, love for, pride in, or gratitude to the receiver of the gift. It isn't a point system.

What if a child asks, "If I am good, can I get this for Christmas?"

Ask him whether Grandma should get a present only if she is good. It is nice to reward people for doing the right thing, but the right thing is what people are supposed to do anyway—give Grandma a gift because you love her.

The Gift of Giving

"I want this," said my son. He was marking off toys in a holiday catalogue in response to a request from his grandmother.

"We can share it," added the other.

"We can share the toys," replied his brother, "but I'm not sharing any underwear."

"Fair enough," I said.

And so it went, page by page, an item here, an item there. One wanting. One sharing. Their list grew longer and their plans all the grander.

"This is too expensive," said one. "But maybe Santa can bring it."

"Maybe," I said as I looked at the price tag. It was doubtful that Santa could swing it this year.

"I like this better," he said.

"And there is a coupon," said the other.

"What does Nana want?" they asked.

"I don't know," I answered. "I haven't asked her yet."

"We should probably find out."

"I'll look for something she might like," said one.

"It can be from both of us," said the other.

And so it went, page by page, an item here, an item there. One pointing out things that others might like. One pointing out things that could be from the both of them.

By the time they were finished, the list of gifts to give was far longer than the list of gifts they wanted to receive.

"I don't think we'll be able to get everything on the lists," I told them.

They retraced their steps, page by page, and when they came to an item here and an item there, one would say, "I don't really want this present."

"I don't want it either," said the other, "but I think that Nana would love it."

And soon the two lists were one, and the boys were proud and happy.

"How is that?" asked my son.

"If we can't buy it, we'll make it," added the other.

"Like an elf," agreed his brother.

Then the catalogue was closed and they went downstairs to play. The sound of laughter bounced recklessly up the stairwell. It was loud and it was sometimes sudden. It was a gift they didn't know they were giving.

And it came from both of them.

Why Your Own Skin Should Be Comfortable

Growing up is part carefree spinning in the summer sun, and part uphill battle of self-imposed insecurity. As parents, we need to make sure our children understand that the awesomeness of others is not the measuring stick with which to gauge our own self-worth. Inspiring? Of course, but not a reflection on the rest of us.

Someone else's fame and good fortune is that person's business, and every child has something fantastic that he brings to the table. Give him the room to find it and the encouragement to embrace it. It's a journey.

TYPICAL PHRASE YOU MAY HEAR: *I wish I was good at something.*

VARIATION: *I'm not good at anything.*

Until they find their "thing," children may experience moments of self-doubt. That is normal, and it doesn't end with childhood—everybody is looking for something.

Once children gain a bit of confidence, they should be able to recognize that the accomplishments of others do not reflect negatively on them, nor do their own accomplishments reflect negatively on anyone else. Gradually, the whole big picture falls into place. Kids get it.

WHAT TO SAY: *Everybody is good at something. You will find yours.*

VARIATION: *You are great at* _____.

It's good to put things in some perspective. Not everyone finds their bliss at the tender age of seven. In fact, most of us take a while to figure out what we want to be when we grow up. Encourage your kid to explore and not to worry about finding something he's good at. He'll discover it when he's ready.

Warning: Some "things" are harder to find than others. Encourage patience and experimentation. Give children space, suggestions, and praise. It is okay to be honest, but do not be critical. Remember, finding their thing doesn't mean that they need to be the best at it; it just means that they love it.

WHAT NOT TO SAY: *You'll never be the best at it.*

VARIATION: *You just aren't very good at* _____.

Seriously. This is the equivalent of telling a kid to give up dreaming, and that is a terrible thing to do. Perhaps saying such things is meant to be helpful and realistic, but encouraging children to give up on a dream is never a good move. Kids will realize their own skill level, aptitude, and enjoyment with this or that activity on their own. They don't need anyone discouraging them from pursuing those pursuits that are still under consideration.

As kids grow more comfortable with trying new things and discovering their own likes and dislikes, they will also gain the confidence to be comfortable in their own skin. Even if they never find their "thing," they may very well find themselves somewhere along the way, and that is pretty good, too.

To Care or Not to Care

Parents can't tell children what they should and shouldn't care about. You can say whatever you want, but your kids are going to—and should—make their own decisions. What you *can* do is provide them with the tools they need to make their way through the onslaught of information hitting them from every direction. It's shouting at their heads and fighting for their fingertips. You can help them negotiate the chaos and find those topics that are directly related to them and their interests. We need to provide our kids with examples that inspire them to develop a sense of perspective. Some things are worth caring more about than others, and our kids deserve to know the difference.

The paradoxical thing is that the same media flooding children with meaningless bits of data—TV and the Internet—are also giving them much of the solid information they need to sort through it.

TYPICAL PHRASE YOU MAY HEAR: *I don't like that show because the kids are mean.*

VARIATION: *They only put toys in their kid meals so we want them, but they aren't good for you.*

What it boils down to is that kids are smart, and despite all the quantities clamoring for their attention, they are still able to recognize quality when they see it. They know when they are being played, and they want to reward those who treat them fairly.

WHAT TO SAY: *What can you do about it?*

VARIATION: *How can you show them you don't like what they are doing?*

Put the ball in the child's court. He understands (or can comprehend after a quick conversation) that by purchasing ads, corporations (sponsors) are paying for the shows we watch, and that those ads target the audience in hopes of selling more products. It sounds complicated, but although kids may not get all the economic angles, they can certainly connect specific products with certain programs or channels that they watch. For instance, when the unhealthy fast-food chain includes toys tied to a hit cartoon, he might decide that the show doesn't care about its audience and remove himself from it. When the tweens on a favorite family show continue to treat adults (parents, principals, teachers) as if they are idiots, despite real-life examples to the contrary, he might decide that someone needs to be held accountable.

TYPICAL PHRASE YOU MAY HEAR: *I'm going to write a letter to complain about it.*

VARIATIONS: *I am not going to watch this show/buy that product.*

WHAT TO SAY: *How can I help?*

VARIATIONS: *I'm proud of you. It's good to take a stand for something you believe in.*

Feels good, doesn't it?

WHAT NOT TO SAY: *Why bother?*

VARIATIONS: *Who cares? You can't change the world. You don't have the power to fix everything.*

Those are the sentiments of someone who has already given up. The kids haven't. Support them in their quest to make sense of it all. Perhaps, in time, they will explain it to us.

A Kid with a Cause

Letting children get involved in citizenship and community service is a fantastic way to increase their awareness of the world, help them find their place in it, and give them opportunities to contribute to the changes they wish to see—all while spending time together meaningfully and enjoyably.

It is a rare and wonderful treat when a child finds something that drives her to passion and subsequent action. It's one thing to recognize a need, and entirely something else to meet it. Should a child find herself so driven, we need to do everything in our power to support and encourage her crusade. It can be downright inspiring.

TYPICAL PHRASE YOU MAY HEAR: *I want to help those kids/people.*

VARIATION: *We can save those animals, trees, rivers, etc.*

Granted, their phrase will be more specific and somewhat more heartfelt, but there is a lot of room for good deeds and citizenship in this world, and the needs that speak to your child may well be among them. Make sure you are listening.

WHAT TO SAY: *That's great! What would you like to do?*

VARIATION: *How can I help?*

This is your kid saving the world, and if you are proud as hell, there is nothing wrong with it. Your child is doing what too many don't, and it is a wonderful thing. Tell your friends. Help in any way you can, but don't forget that this is *her* passion, and you are in a supporting role. Encourage her to lead by example and to get other kids involved. A movement has to start somewhere.

TYPICAL PHRASE YOU MAY HEAR: *I want to help, but I'm just a kid.*

VARIATION: *I'm only one person.*

This is where you can play a huge role. Find examples in the news, in history, in literature, in the movies, or anywhere on the Internet of young people in action. There are many inspiring kids out there doing humbling work, and any one of them should help quiet whatever self-doubt your child may harbor on her path to action. Don't let her give up without ever trying.

Once she understands that anybody can make a difference, regardless of how small, she'll be off and running. All it takes is dedication, hard work, and a parent to drive her around, maybe pay for lunch.

WHAT NOT TO SAY: *Just worry about yourself.*

VARIATIONS: *That isn't our problem. Someone else will worry about it.*

Thankfully, our kids are smarter than we are. Let them do what they feel is right, and you will see a beautiful transformation in how they carry themselves and how they interact with the world.

All You Need Is Love

Most people believe that we live in a culture where our differences—whether in ethnicity, religion, political beliefs, diet, sexual orientation, or favorite sports team—actually make us better as a whole. Even so, there are plenty of people who don't share this belief. That can make things awkward for the rest of the world. However, I am convinced that we're moving toward a more caring society, and our kids have a lot to do with it. Your job is to teach tolerance and inclusiveness, making it clear that you're for a society that cares and gives people a choice about their lifestyle.

TYPICAL PHRASE YOU MAY HEAR: *Why does Jimmy have two dads?*

VARIATION: *How did Jimmy's dads have him?*

With many states (and the federal government) starting to recognize the right of same-sex couples to marry, kids are sure to meet a wider range of family types and will ask you questions about them. There is a good chance this has already happened to you, in regard to either your own family or someone close to you.

WHAT TO SAY: *Some kids have a mommy and daddy, some kids have two daddies or two mommies, and some kids have one parent or more than two. Everybody's family is different, and that is what makes them special. If all families were the same, life would be boring. It isn't important what kind of parents kids have, as long as they have kind parents.*

VARIATIONS: *It was a little harder for Jimmy's dads to have him—there is a bunch of expensive legal stuff involved. Here is what it boils down to: The daddies had so much love that they needed to share it with someone, and who better than a child? I don't know the details of how they met Jimmy—that is their story to tell—but they did, and they are all better because of it.*

Whether you want to take your conversation down the paths of explaining adoption or surrogacy is up to you, but kids know what love is, and they respect it as an answer—that goes for most questions.

WHAT NOT TO SAY: *You can't play with Jimmy. We don't approve of his parents' immoral lifestyle.*

Open bigotry and hate are rapidly declining in our society, but sadly, in many places and among many people they are still alive and kicking. As parents, you need to do your best to see that such hurtful attitudes go the way of the dodo.

There is a long list of things not to say and words not to use. Most of them involve inflicting various degrees of ignorance and hate on the next generation. Don't do that.

YOU'VE GOT TO BE CAREFULLY TAUGHT

Rodgers and Hammerstein received a lot of backlash over their Broadway show tune "You've Got to Be Carefully Taught" from the hit 1949 musical *South Pacific*. Mostly because it was true. The song was cued by a line stating that racism is "not born in you. It happens after you are born"—and then the crowd went wild.

The lyrics suggest that people "hate all the people your relatives hate" due to conditioning by family and society, and that "you've got to be taught to hate and fear."

Needless to say, when the show reached the stage in the still-segregated state of Georgia, the outrage was so loud that a bill was introduced to outlaw expressing such a sentiment, claiming that it was a direct threat to the American way of life.

Basically, Georgia lawmakers went to a lot of trouble to prove Rodgers and Hammerstein were right.

These days, open racism, sexism, and homophobia are not nearly as prevalent in the United States as they once were. But hate still exists, and it's uncomfortably vocal in sharing its ignorance. That kind of hateful thought starts in the home, but it can just as easily end there. See that it does.

It's Not a Race

The human race is broken down into many subsections because everybody loves a label. However, despite what differences we have, we are all, at our core, one and the same.

We all love, fear, laugh, cry, and everything else that makes us human. It is ridiculous to believe that some people are different because of the shade of their skin. Yet this sort of ignorance does persist—alarmingly so—in our society today.

TYPICAL PHRASE YOU MAY HEAR: *Jimmy's mom said that he should stay away from [insert ethnicity] people.*

VARIATION: *All of the jokes Uncle Dwayne tells make fun of [insert ethnicity] people.*

Your first instinct may be to tell your kid he can't play with Jimmy, except that doesn't solve the problem, it ignores it. Also, what the hell, Uncle Dwayne?

The problem with bigots and racists (besides the obvious harm they do) is that they are often under the misconception that others agree with their distorted world view or, at the very least, find their so-called humor funny. This is where *we* can make a difference. Instead of ignoring such behavior, or justifying it on the basis of age, lack of education, or whatever other excuse we can find, let's challenge it every time it arises. We may or may not change their minds, but we can probably shut them up a bit, and that is nice, too.

WHAT TO SAY: *Jimmy's mom is wrong. [Insert ethnicity] people aren't any different from the rest of us.*

VARIATION: *Next time Uncle Dwayne tells a joke like that, tell him that he is not funny, he is offensive.*

Sure, let your kid shame Uncle Dwayne. It might knock him back a step or two and make him realize how inappropriate his jokes are in general, especially in front of someone impressionable who, for better or worse, looks up to him.

Obviously, you'll need to make some phone calls to the various adults in these scenarios, and those will probably be awkward. However, the alternative is to allow adults, people whom your child trusts, to abuse their influence and make unacceptable things seem acceptable.

WHAT NOT TO SAY: *You should always stay away from strangers.*

VARIATION: *They are just jokes.*

Of course you want your child to be aware of the potential dangers that lurk in our society, and rules against stranger interaction should be established to guard against that. But when you warn your children about being wary of strangers in the context of this particular discussion, it only serves to validate the original comment by Jimmy's mom. You hear yourself saying "stranger," but your child hears "_____ people are strange."

Jokes that exploit and reinforce negative stereotypes of anyone (whether in terms of ethnicity, gender, religion, physical prowess, learning ability, or sexual orientation) offer nothing positive for a child. Uncle Dwayne might have told those jokes without malice, and some of them might even be funny, but a child won't understand the subtext required to distinguish such implications from reality, and there is nothing funny about that.

CHAPTER 3

Life and Death: Death Is the Downside and There Will Be Questions

There are a number of things we never want to talk about with our children. Sex and drugs get a lot publicity, but those are, for the most part, temporary bumps on the timeline. Death is at the end of it, and to a child who knows nothing but life and the wonders of it, that is a tough idea to comprehend.

There are many faces of death, and twice as many ways to talk about it. None of them are fun. Some people use religion as a guide; others use science and nature. Some sell death as the first step to someplace better, and others dwell on the finality of it all. The fact is that all the way through adulthood, we struggle with the concept.

Timing is also important, since parents often wait until death is happening to broach the subject with kids. In such cases your family might actually be suffering from loss during the conversation. This adds to the emotional force of the moment, and our own pain makes death all the more powerful and frightening to them.

There is no easy way to talk about death. But some ways are easier than others.

Death in the News

The media make death, as a topic, first and foremost. Sometimes it seems as if it's the main point in every other story they share, and sometimes they even manage to act like they care more about the human element than selling the sound bite. It's all very touching.

However, constant exposure to news about death may desensitize those children who pay attention to such things. The more death they see, the more normal it seems to be. After a while, they stop paying attention.

Other children take each reported death as the tragedy that it is and are overwhelmed by the sadness of it all. As parents, your job is to find some type of middle ground between the two.

The media take matters a step further and focuses on the reasons behind the death. In an attempt to report every shred of news, they often create celebrity caricatures of killers and criminals, pumping life into nightmares and boogeymen.

TYPICAL PHRASE YOU MAY HEAR: *Why did that person kill somebody?*

VARIATIONS: *Why did they want to kill people? Why did that man want to hurt someone?*

This is advanced stuff. Obviously every news story affects us all differently. Some acts of violence, though not justifiable, are easier to explain—at the very least we can attach them to wars, mental illness, accidents, or misguided belief systems. The media usually handle those labels for us.

WHAT TO SAY: *Some people believe that the only way to make their point is to hurt others. They are wrong.*

VARIATION: *Some people get angry, confused, or scared, and they do bad things out of desperation.*

While these answers are appropriate to the child's questions, you should be aware that neither is going to put your child's mind at ease. That's because they aren't answering the questions children are *really* asking. Sure, the words came out of their mouth, but what they really want to know is why did such a thing happen *and* will it happen to them?

WHAT TO SAY: *Those terrible things are not normal.*

VARIATION: *You are safe.*

Safe is, obviously, relative, but it is also true. This is the most important point on which to reassure your child. She is as safe as she could ever be, and that lets us sleep at night. It is the best we can do, and there should be solace in that. Apply hugs as needed.

WHAT NOT TO SAY: *Accidents happen.*

VARIATION: *Some people just like hurting others.*

This may be chalked up to semantics, but suggesting that "accidents happen" implies the vague possibility that accidents will happen to them. There is no way to guarantee that accidents won't happen to your children, but there is also no reason to put unnecessary fears into their little heads.

Saying that "some people like hurting others" will only cause nightmares—and those can wait until the kids are older. The main thing is to reinforce the message that you're making your child as safe as you possibly can, and that you love her.

Losing a Relative

If life were fair, most kids would never lose a relative until their grandparents and others of that generation were deep into their golden years. But life is not fair, and although older family members are likely to be the first of a child's relatives to die, there is no guarantee that will be the case. Life is full of surprises, and some of them are tragically sad and hard to understand. These are the holes that never entirely fill, and it is our job to make sure the kids don't suffer so badly that they cannot recover.

Most adults, by the time they are parents, have lost a relative, and they understand the pain and loss involved. Kids, although they are able to comprehend that death is an end, lack the ability to understand the implications of it. That is, they don't know what it is like to go for years missing someone whose presence they once took for granted. No amount of explanation on our part can entirely prepare them for this kind of loss. All we can do is be there when they need us.

TYPICAL PHRASE YOU MAY HEAR: *Will I ever see them again?*

VARIATION: *Will they be in Heaven?*

These questions might be somewhat easier to answer for those whose belief system is built on the promise of such things, that doesn't mean that kids—or anyone else, for that matter— like the idea of a lifetime without those they love.

WHAT TO SAY: *Everything you love about them will always be with you. As long as you remember them, they will live inside you.*

VARIATION: *You will see them again in Heaven (or the version of afterlife that you believe in).*

Those who don't believe in any form of afterlife should stick with the first reply.

TYPICAL PHRASE YOU MAY HEAR: *Why did they have to die?*

Associating a reason with death makes the process slightly easier to explain, especially with regard to illness or some other tragic situation wherein the deceased was obviously suffering. To accept something such as cancer, however, can sometimes feel like giving in to it, and a child should be made aware of the difference.

WHAT TO SAY: *They were very sick and they were in a lot of pain. Now they don't have to suffer any longer.*

Sometimes the answers are harder to sell to ourselves than to the kids.

WHAT NOT TO SAY: *Everything happens for a reason.*

VARIATION: *The Lord works in mysterious ways.*

This is a cop-out to avoid telling children the hard truth. Show them that you respect them enough to give them real answers, even if you need to water these answers down to age-appropriate levels.

STANDING AGAINST CANCER

Accepting the loss of a loved one to cancer may be unavoidable and necessary, but letting cancer get away with it is something entirely different. Many people, children included, find that fighting against the disease in question—by raising money and awareness—is a wonderful way to respect the deceased, and also to increase the chance that others will not experience a similar tragedy. This is the positive to be found in a bad situation, and letting kids throw a few figurative punches in the gut of cancer feels pretty darn good.

Losing a Friend

Most children will go deep into their teens, or even their twenties, before losing a friend to illness, accident, or other tragedy. Bereavement is never easy, but losing someone of a similar age during the earlier years of personal development can drastically scar a child's psyche. It is very common for children to need professional assistance in order to cope and move on. Losing a friend makes death very, very real.

One of the effects, which is a very natural reaction for children, is to worry that whatever befell their friend might also happen to them. Don't take this as a lack of sympathy or sadness; rather, it's an extension of it. What happened to their friend scares them, and fear has a way of spreading.

TYPICAL PHRASE YOU MAY HEAR: *How could someone so young die?*

VARIATIONS: *She was too young to die. Why did he have to die now?*

How do you respond to this? Of course the child was too young, and while the "how" might be easier to explain in terms of the science of it, the real questions is the "why," and nobody can answer that.

WHAT TO SAY: *I don't know.*

There, you said it. Under normal circumstances, the fact that you don't know all the answers might be a blow to your god-like parenting status, but in this situation it isn't about what you know, but what you do. Hug your kids and don't let them go for as long as humanly possible.

It is important that you allow your children time to grieve, but also keep a close eye on them. The sadness of losing a friend can take children into some pretty dark areas, and we need to make sure that their grief, terrible as it is, does not linger too long. Check on them often. Be there for them always. And if it's indicated, seek professional assistance for them.

WHAT NOT TO SAY: *That could have been you.*

In the rare case (such as a traffic accident) when that phrase is true, it should still remain unspoken. Your object is *not* to scare your kid further; quite the opposite. You may find yourself at least thinking that statement, if not saying it aloud, as part of your own shock and grieving—people can't help but project the what-ifs of tragedy onto their own reality. It is human nature.

But if a child hears you say that, it could start wheels spinning that should be still.

On the chance that there is a real lesson to be taken from the death of a friend—for example, both children were involved in a situation that resulted in an accident—then, carefully, discuss it with your child. Most likely he is acutely aware of how close to death he came and will want to talk with you about it.

Losing a Pet

One of the earliest and purist bonds that children form is with the family pet, and because of the considerably shorter lifespan of most domesticated animals, losing a pet is likely to be their first real exposure to death on a personal level. It isn't pretty.

Some people have difficulty equating the loss of a pet with that of the loved ones covered elsewhere in this section. In typical situations, the death of the family dog may not warrant the same level of grief as that of a friend or relative. However, it isn't just the pain of the death that makes losing a pet so difficult, but also the very real and obvious hole left in the child's daily routine.

The pet was not just a loved one. In many cases, having a pet was also the child's first experience with responsibility (feeding, exercising, etc.). In addition to the sadness of losing a friend, confidant, and well-loved companion, there is also the emptiness left when that responsibility is no longer theirs.

TYPICAL PHRASE YOU MAY HEAR: *I was supposed to take care of her! Is it my fault she died?*

VARIATION: *Did I do something wrong?*

Depending on the type of pet and the duties involved, there may or may not be some validity to these questions, but unless the child literally killed the pet with malicious intent (in which case, professional help is indicated), we should spare them any guilt that might be associated with their performance. (That's not to say we can't help them with their "pet skills" to ensure a higher survival rate in future animals.)

WHAT TO SAY: *It is not your fault. You loved her, and that is all anyone could ask for.*

VARIATION: *She had a good life, and that is because of you.*

Let's not make this any harder than it needs to be.

WHAT NOT TO SAY: *Yes, it was your fault.*

VARIATION: *You killed her.*

You just made it harder.

Although the immediate impact of the death may be great, it is in the time following the death that sadness really takes its toll. It is not uncommon for children to ask about a deceased pet weeks, months, or even years after its passing.

TYPICAL PHRASE YOU MAY HEAR: *I miss her.*

As with the death of any loved one, children need to be able to express their continued sorrow and share their memories with others. You should encourage your children to think about their loss not only with sadness, but also with happiness when they remember what joy the pet's life brought. Reflect upon the dead with fondness.

WHAT TO SAY: *That's because you loved her, and you still do.*

Death in the Movies

These days, movies aimed at children and families have a surprising amount of death in them. Some of the more popular films in the genre are famous for killing off parents—sometimes before the opening credits are over—and then building their story around the subsequent coming of age that follows (Harry Potter, I'm looking at you). There is probably a well-researched marketing principle behind this; perhaps sadness is directly related to the selling of popcorn—who knows? Whatever the rationale, there is a lot of death in the movies, and our kids are washing it down with their bodyweight in soda.

Fortunately, despite the deadly plot lines, the percentage of young children who lose a parent in reality is relatively small. And there are actually many lessons we can all learn from films like this. Films that have loss as a component of their story can help teach children to overcome adversity and tragedy, and live their lives to the fullest. After all, the best way to honor the dead is by living.

The reaction that death scenes most commonly evoke in children is fear.

TYPICAL PHRASE YOU MAY HEAR: *I was scared when the daddy died.*

VARIATION: *Why did the mommy die?*

Good question. Maybe you were scared, too. Movies may not be real, but they sure feel like it while you are watching them. Luckily, there is nothing wrong with a bit of fear.

WHAT TO SAY: *It was scary, but it was just a movie and none of it was real.*

VARIATIONS: *It was just a story that someone made up using her or his imagination. Nobody really died.*

If the film provides children with a trial run at death and fear, then the soothing that follows serves a similar purpose for parents. Never take this sort of thing for granted. Chances are you'll have to explain a real death to your kid someday. It's better to start with one that's not real.

WHAT NOT TO SAY: *People die.*

VARIATION: *Parents die all the time.*

While technically correct, the statement that we are all going to die should not be the message that sticks with the child. The time for fear was during the film; now it's time to talk about it.

Find out why, exactly, the child was scared. Was she frightened of facing death herself? Was she scared that you or her other parent is going to die and leave her alone? Or did the movie scene touch on some real-life experience she has had? There are lots of reasons why a child might be frightened by death in a movie, and it then becomes our role to hear her out and do our best to put her mind at ease.

Sometimes these conversations go best over ice cream.

THE BENEFIT OF SCARY MOVIES

While a great number of people look to film too often for role models, the cinema does provide useful opportunities to address otherwise delicate topics in a manufactured and fictionalized environment. For instance, kids need to know what scary feels like, and it is much better for them to first recognize it in a quiet theater with their parents by their side than in real situations.

Fear is an emotion like any other, and children need to experience it as they develop their sense of self and personal growth. If that experience is rooted in two-hour blocks of entertainment rather than in reality, all the better. Preparing for fear does not mean you are courting it.

Carpe Diem!

Despite the shocking amount of death that kids face on a daily basis (see previous entries), they remain amazingly resilient and comfortable in the belief that mortality does not apply to them. They have seen death, but they have felt life, and they know which one they like better. The future is blurry, but today is clear and bright. *Now*, as a concept, will last for always.

TYPICAL PHRASE YOU MAY HEAR: *I want to live forever.*

VARIATION: *Nothing can hurt me!*

Ah, to be young and invincible. It is actually a pretty impressive thing to watch, and this makes it all the harder to ensure that children understand the limits of life and respect them. However, that's part of your job as a parent.

WHAT TO SAY: *Living forever is overrated. Live for today!*

VARIATION: *Remember when you slammed your fingers in the car door? That looked like it hurt.*

There is no better combination in the parenting playbook than humor and tenderness. A dash of either is always a nice touch, but together they can drive any message home.

Regarding the idea that nothing can hurt them, a simple reminder should suffice to prove the contrary—or just wait ten minutes. Something else will come along.

Clearly, you could go into more serious detail about the dangers of life and the safety precautions it requires, but that just adds unneeded stress and fear. Stuff can hurt them. They remember now.

There would be some real drawbacks to living forever. This is an opening to discuss downsides with your child. Your examples of wrinkles, adult diapers, impaired vision and hearing, and other forms of decline in old age will go a long way in helping children rethink an endless timeline. Living in the now is where it's at.

WHAT NOT TO SAY: *Nothing lives forever; we are all going to die.*

VARIATIONS: *Everything can hurt you. You need to be careful.*

Pounding it home that the world is full of pain and destruction is not necessarily the best way to explain mortality to children. Scare tactics may inspire too much caution. The fact that life is short and sometimes dangerous should make it all the more sweet and precious, not something to hide from. Seize the day, kids!

TYPICAL PHRASE YOU MAY HEAR: *Let's do something!*

This may not sound much like a comment on the shortness of life, but take it as such. At the very least, consider that the window of childhood is incredibly small, and these opportunities are available for a limited time only. Make the most of them.

WHAT TO SAY: *Let's do it!*

It doesn't matter what "it" is. You are doing it together, and nobody is getting any younger. Do as much as you can, and do it together.

WHAT NOT TO SAY: *Not now. We'll do something later.*

You probably won't, and even if you *do* do the proverbial "something" later, there is still an opportunity missed and one less memory made. DVR the sports game. *That* is the stuff you can do later.

THE WISDOM OF SHAWSHANK

In Stephen King's novella *The Shawshank Redemption*, which was later made into a fantastic movie starring Morgan Freeman and Tim Robbins, the character Red (Freeman) says at one point, "Get busy living, or get busy dying."

Words to live by—and, one day, to die by. Assuming we do well by the former, then the latter should be all the more peaceful.

Live each day to the fullest, take chances, and make the most of the time you have. If you impart that wisdom to your children, everyone will be better for it.

Accepting Mortality

There will come a time when children start to accept their own mortality, or at least to acknowledge it. Some kids take it better than others, but none of them like it. Can you blame them?

They will have similar epiphanies about us, their parents, as well as other family members. It hits like a ton of bricks.

The catalyst for their discovery might be the death of a loved one, something they heard from a friend, a conversation with you, or a Sunday sermon. In the end, it doesn't really matter how or why they start asking questions about mortality. What counts is that we are there to talk with them about it.

TYPICAL PHRASE YOU MAY HEAR: *Am I going to die?*

VARIATIONS: *Are you going to die? Is Grandma going to die?*

Have a seat. This may hurt a bit.

There is really only one answer here. It is the delivery that matters. Like most scenarios in this book, this one is guided by the personalities of those involved, the sensitivities of the child, and his or her general awareness of death.

Let the child guide the conversation. It's tough because, unlike other situations we've covered, all paths lead to the same destination: Yes, we are all going to die. There is no alternative, but there is also no rush. Your child will have questions and so will you. That's okay. As far as topics of conversation go, this is a big one.

WHAT TO SAY: *Yes, some day, which is why today is so special.*

VARIATION: *There is nothing we can do about dying, but there's plenty to be done about living.*

These responses might sound somewhat cheesy or slightly clichéd, but that doesn't make them any less true. One solid point to consider is that dying, in itself, is not a bad or evil thing. Yes, it is terribly sad and often tragic, but it's also the end we know is coming.

Spinning this into a conversation that a child can understand and accept, however, may prove a tall order.

WHAT NOT TO SAY: *No, we aren't going to die.*

VARIATIONS: *Let's not talk about this. It's too depressing.*

Unless you mean we're not likely to die in the next few minutes, there isn't a lot of wiggle room with this question, and it won't be long before the kid calls you on it. He will probably understand that you were just trying to protect him or make him feel better, so your untruth may not scar him forever, but sometimes it is just better to give it to him straight. There is a reason why people say the truth hurts, and you're living it.

The Undead, and Making the Most of Second Chances

The undead are back, and most of them are much more popular this time around—vampires and zombies and ghosts, oh my!

TV shows, movies, books, you name it: The horror genre has gone mainstream, and we are all eating it up like so many brains. The kids are loving it, too.

The question is, does such reanimation desensitize children even further to the concept of death? Does it scare them with new possibilities or even register at all?

Do the undead make death cool? If so, is there anything wrong with that?

TYPICAL PHRASE YOU MAY HEAR: *I wish I was dead.*

VARIATION: *I want to be a vampire.*

The former is a lot more important, immediately, than the latter. The chances of someone actually becoming a vampire are pretty slim, but dying is much more realistic, and to hear it come from a child's mouth, even in the context of role-playing and fantasy, gives us pause, as well it should.

WHAT TO SAY: *Do you understand what you are saying?*

Give them a moment to realize what they are saying, and depending on their response, proceed accordingly.

If they mean it as a stepping-stone to becoming a vampire, make sure they understand that the likelihood of such a transformation actually happening is never. Then reiterate why the statement sets off alarms and that they should avoid making it.

If they are confused about the lines between the undead and reality, then perhaps they should watch something else—after a very thorough conversation examining the topic(s).

WHAT NOT TO SAY: *Don't ever say that!*

Even though you are justified in feeling the concern implied in this response, it only adds to the mystery and coolness factor if you don't back up your statement with clear reasoning that your child can understand. After all, how many vampires listen to their parents?

There is nothing wrong with enjoying the spooky side of death, but children need to understand where the fun stops and more serious matters begin.

PART II

In the Home

CHAPTER 4

Play and Creativity: Enter the Imagination

When was the last time you played or did something creative just for the fun of it—not because your kid wanted to, not because it was an enjoyable way to burn some calories, and not because the team-building exercise at work required trust and crayons. Just unadulterated, big-grin fun, like no one was watching?

Is the answer making you sad?

Sorry about that.

You don't have to ask a kid about *her* last experience of random and spontaneous enjoyment, because she's doing it right now—or, rather, she was until you stopped the fun to ask her if she was having any.

Live in the now, parents.

That is all kids ever do when we aren't bending them to the seriousness of our existence. They play. They create. They eat. They poop. They sleep. Being a kid isn't nearly as hard as we remember, and it is twice as fleeting.

With few exceptions and despite every claim to the contrary, we adults no longer live within the world of children's imagination. We're just lucky if we can visit once in a while.

Your kid will be happy to show you around.

SAY GOODBYE TO CHILDHOOD

One of the greatest gifts that we as parents will ever receive from our children is an open invitation to playtime. Unfortunately, we are often too busy or otherwise occupied to make the most of our golden ticket. Consider what we are missing: If you took the ending of A.A. Milne's *The House at Pooh Corner*, the goodbye strip of Bill Watterson's *Calvin and Hobbes*, and Harry Chapin's "Cat's in the Cradle" in its melancholy entirety, and then mixed them all together in the pocket of a favorite shirt that your kid grew out of . . . well, you see where this is going.

Now let's get out there and enjoy their childhood before it is gone.

We're Going to Need a Bigger Refrigerator

Kids are born artists. The world is their canvas, and life is their medium. We were like that, too. Once. Now we are the curators of a pint-sized gallery, and the artists are restless. There better be snacks and chilled juice boxes at the opening. No apple!

This embrace of the creative, along with blatant disregard for form (and sometimes content), is one of the greatest gifts of childhood. Kids don't realize it because it is all they know, but *we* know. We know.

The problem then isn't the act of putting imagination on paper, but rather the nonstop results—kids make a lot of projects, and frankly, some of them are better than others. We may not know art, but we know what will impress people who look at our refrigerators.

TYPICAL PHRASE YOU MAY HEAR: *Do you like my drawing?*

VARIATIONS: *Is this a good picture? Do you like what I made?*

Is it a flamingo in the snow or a candy cane melting on the beach? It is whatever they say it is.

WHAT TO SAY: *Yes.*

You say, "Yes." *Every. Single. Time.* Then you back it up with all the praise, raves, and encouragement that you can muster (use a thesaurus). Look how well it worked out for Jackson Pollock. The refrigerator in his childhood home must have been covered in awesome.

WHAT NOT TO SAY: *No.*

VARIATIONS: *You can do better. I don't like it. It's not good. Wouldn't it have been better if you had . . .*

I suppose there is some Bizarro World where people think that offering negative criticism of a child's creativity is doing her a favor, what with tough love and all that, but how is making a child ashamed of her imagination doing anything positive for anyone?

Maybe you're not an "art person," which is (a) sad or (b) whatever makes you feel better. But creating art isn't just about creating a thing of beauty and a joy forever—it is about expanding the mind, the grasp of knowledge, and the lens through which we view the world. The creative process is an expression of the imagination. It is finding ways to appreciate the beauty, details, and wonder of life. Art is mighty, and it is both the pen and the sword.

Oh, is this your soapbox?

Still don't like the drawing? Remember, just because your child makes a piece of art doesn't mean that you have to display it. Sometimes things can be "saved for posterity," and that is open to interpretation.

All you have to do is say "yes" and smile. Their imagination will do the rest.

WHERE ART THOU?

Kids, understandably, don't want to throw away any of their art, whether it was crafted over six months under intense artistic tutelage or scribbled over nachos on the kid's menu at Chili's.

Parents will find the process becomes easier over time.

There are a number of ways to "keep" as much of their art as you see fit without actually covering the surface of every kitchen appliance or wallpapering the entire house with it (although that's an interesting option). For example, there are websites and apps that enable parents to create a virtual gallery of their child's art. There is also the spirit of giving, which means putting the collective masterpieces in a big envelope and sending them to relatives—add a tasteful frame and you have a wonderful gift.

Physical storage works, too, but you are only delaying the inevitable.

I Learned It from Watching You, Okay?

Kids are like monkeys, and not just in the sense that they carry every disease in existence, but also in the much nicer "monkey see, monkey do" spin on our evolutionary cousins. Children copy the behavior they see, and they see that behavior at home—watching us.

That is a lot of power for any one person to wield, and most of us aren't taking advantage of the situation. We yell and we eat poorly. We watch trashy TV and pretend our four-year-old is three if it will save us ninety bucks on a theme park ticket. We do these things without a lot of thought, and we tend to forget that every single action is being absorbed by the small, smiling sponge holding our hand, waiting for his time to come. Someday he too will yell at the server because the fries are too salty, just like Mom and Dad! That's on us.

Luckily, we can make amends. To paraphrase Gandhi, be the example you wish to see in your children.

It's not really as deep as all that. For example, if you want to stress the importance and wonder of reading to children, then don't tell them about it; show them. Open books and turn their pages for hours at a time.

Paint, play an instrument, work in the garden, shoot baskets—whatever it is that you think is super-awesome, do it. Remember, kids are much more likely to do what they see than what they are told.

TYPICAL PHRASE YOU MAY HEAR: *I don't want to read! I want to watch TV with you!*

VARIATION: *I don't want to play outside! I want to play on the computer like you!*

Do you notice the theme? Kids want to do things like their parents and *with* their parents. We should seize every opportunity to introduce our children to good habits, incredible activities, and all the things we always mean to do before it is too late.

WHAT TO SAY: *I'm going to read, too. Grab a book and come sit by me.*

VARIATION: *I'll go outside with you. What do you want to play?*

Easy, right? These are the moments when seeds are planted, and these are the moments we will miss most as our children grow up.

WHAT NOT TO SAY: *Do as I say, not as I do.*

VARIATION: *When you're a grownup, you can do whatever you want.*

These are two popular responses to children in many different situations, and they are never the right one. When we invoke them, we're negating our value as role models, and as parents we should be *the* role model for our children. Also, while the second negative response is true to some extent, it overlooks the fact that adult responsibilities often constrain the choices of adults. Moreover, that glib answer reinforces the idea that the activity you want them to pursue is not fun or desirable but rather something they can someday escape just by aging. And don't forget when they go *that* route they are taking their childhood with them. What's the hurry?

Shall We Play a Game?

We live in a time of such rapid advancements in the field of video gaming that our children have never known the thrill of playing Pong or standing in line for Space Invaders in the video arcade, clutching warm, sweaty quarters in their tightly squeezed hands. That was living, man!

These days every phone is a gaming system, and every kid has a phone (or something comparable) in his or her pocket. The future is awesome!

Have you met George Jetson yet?

As in nearly everything else, there are positive and negative side effects of playing video games. Parents, being the wise and logical people that we invariably are, have opinions in both camps. Despite that, kids do not want to hear about our misgivings. They saw outside yesterday, and it seemed fine.

TYPICAL PHRASE YOU MAY HEAR: *Drink milk after you eat a zombie and you will heal faster.*

VARIATIONS: *Creepers are afraid of cats. Come like my igloo.*

Just kidding. Sort of. Those are things kids say when they are playing Minecraft and Club Penguin, respectively, and there is not a proper response because you have no idea what they are talking about. It's okay; go back to whatever you were doing.

TYPICAL PHRASE YOU MAY HEAR: *May I download this game?*

VARIATION: *Can I buy an upgrade?*

No matter how many games kids may have, and they have a lot, they will always want more. That's just the way it is. It is Greedy Kid 101, now available for iPad, but don't say that aloud or they will want to buy *it*, too.

WHAT TO SAY: *Have you cleaned your room?*

VARIATION: *Have you completed your other games?*

At first glance those two replies may seem very different, but the gist is the same: Have pre-existing requirements in place, and feed their rabid addiction to gaming as a reward for fulfilling whatever those prerequisites may be. It's okay; gaming is fun and they love it, so let them enjoy it within whatever time constraints and other rules you choose to set. The desire for new games and/or upgrades is insatiable, and you may as well harness it for your teachable moments. That's Resourceful Parenting 101 (also available at graduate level).

WHAT NOT TO SAY: *Okay.*

VARIATION: *Whatever.*

That's not to suggest that you shouldn't treat a kid to something she wants just for the heck of it once in a while, but keep in mind that not every game or app is intended for children— and even those that are aimed at their demographic may not be in their best interests. Take a minute to acquaint yourself with whatever it is they are interested in, and make the call accordingly.

ARE VIDEO GAMES GOOD FOR KIDS?

You have seen the theories, articles, and reports about the benefits of gaming, which include improvements to literacy, decision-making, vision, motor skills, reflexes, coordination, and dexterity, all of which seems to make a lot of sense. It has also been said that playing video games reduces pain, stress, and depression and that it counters stereotypes of gender differences. Those claims run a pretty wide gamut.

The negative side effects of gaming are more readily evident. For example, all that gamut running isn't providing one gigabyte of exercise. Also, extended game play may result in behavioral and anger issues, as well as sapping interest in other activities.

Both benefits and drawbacks will vary, but if you're looking for peace of mind regarding the former, you've found it. For more information, check out *www.abcnews.go.com/blogs/technology/2011/12/the-benefits-of-video-games* and *www.health.yahoo.net/experts/dayinhealth/surprising-health-benefits-video-games.*

There Is a Monster at the End of This Game

His face was a soft scowl beneath sun-kissed golden hair. His eyes were heavy with lash and pout. He willed a drop of cold sweat, and felt nothing but a tingle where the shakes should be.

It wasn't an addiction to a life-threatening substance, but it was an addiction all the same. He *needed* video games, and the agony and anger that festered upon their withdrawal caused his parents great concern and occasioned much discussion. Neither of which was received with an ounce of appreciation.

Sean made promises to his parents—and didn't keep them. He worked out deals—and quickly defaulted on them. Each time, his parents, David and

Sarah, gave him the benefit of the doubt. And each time, he let them down.

Finally, they'd had it. They took away the video game console. David wanted to sell the lot, including a ton of games and accessories, to the highest bidder he could find on the Internet. He was outvoted by a game-loving Sarah and Sean's younger brother, who didn't deserve to be deprived because of his brother's difficulties.

There was a precedent for David and Sarah's actions. The previous year the system was broken for months. During that time, Sean morphed from an eight-year-old emo kid back into the laughing boy they had once known.

Then, when the game system became available again, he resumed the slow descent into the seedy underbelly of video game addiction.

The descent proceeded so slowly that his parents were not certain it was actually happening. He made excuses. He was tired. His brother was pestering him. Sarah and David wanted to believe.

But that sweet, sensitive boy was becoming a monster. He yelled and screamed at both those who played with him and those who told him it was time to stop. He talked in quick, sharp daggers of hateful speech, and he whined when his parents mentioned the problem. It was ugly.

The time allotted to playing video games was already very little. Sean was able to play only on the weekends and for a set amount of time per session. When his behavior again became an issue those windows began to close, and eventually they slammed shut.

The kid had had every warning and every chance in the world.

"Sean," his father said to him, "we've tried to be fair, but you're not giving us an alternative. We're removing your video privileges completely and taking away your games."

"It's not *fair!*" Sean shouted angrily.

David sighed. "I'm sorry you feel that way," he replied, "but that's our decision. If you want your privileges back, we're going to have to see a big change in your behavior."

After Sarah and David took away the system, they had to endure days of endless complaining. Sean cursed the world and let it weigh upon his shoulders. Although he hadn't played video games in weeks, he still craved his fix. This time his behavior hadn't changed in the way his parents hoped.

Perhaps it was time for therapy.

Pop Culture Invasion II: What Comes Around Goes Around and the Benefits Thereof

There are a lot of milestones in a child's life, and one of the biggest involves two of the most controversial questions we must answer as parents: At what age do we show our children the *Star*

Wars movies? And do we screen them in chronological order of story line or by theater release date?

Seriously, this is very important.

As your children get older, you will face similar dilemmas with the *Lord of the Rings* and *Hobbit* films.

For the record, there are worse problems.

Like most generations, we believe that we are living in the golden age of pop culture, and to an extent that is true. We currently have all that is new and wonderful, as well as those gems that have stood the test of time and remain firmly entrenched in polite society. For example, kids today are growing up with access to the Stooges, the Beatles, and *The Avengers*—and they have it all at their fingertips wherever they may go.

The only thing that can surpass today is tomorrow, but for the purposes of this conversation, let's stay in the now.

One of the best things about childhood, from the outside looking in, is that we, the parents, are able to share our passions with a captive audience and subsequently bend them toward our views on music, TV, movies, and literature. Granted, children might decide they like something else as they get older, which is fine, but chances are that at least for a while, they will relish the things that we cherish, and that, right there, is a fantastic feeling.

Not that they owe us anything.

TYPICAL PHRASE YOU MAY HEAR: *Han shot first.*

VARIATION: *I am the walrus.*

Congratulations. You are doing it right.

WHAT TO SAY: *They only edited* Star Wars *because Han Solo is a hero, and heroes don't go around killing people. It's a noble goal, but the arc of Han Solo's character is lessened greatly by the change.*

VARIATION: *John Lennon based the walrus on a character from Lewis Carroll's poem "The Walrus and the Carpenter," which is from the book* Through the Looking Glass. *When he wrote the song, Lennon mistook the walrus for a hero.*

Okay, you may not answer exactly like that, but that is just an example of the deep conversations that parents can enjoy with their children when finding common ground in pop culture. It's good bonding.

WHAT NOT TO SAY: *You shouldn't care so much about that stuff.*

VARIATION: *I thought the walrus was Paul.*

Seriously, you should be ashamed of yourself.

That said, there will be plenty of instances where parents and children disagree on the coolness of this show or that band—don't let that come between you. Children are their own people, and parents should make every attempt to support and understand whatever it is that the kids are into these days.

HAN SHOT FIRST!

The phrase "Han shot first" is in reference to Han Solo, the *Star Wars* character played by Harrison Ford. An updated version of *Star Wars Episode IV: A New Hope* (the original *Star Wars* film), which was re-released in 1997, changed a scene between Han Solo and the bounty hunter Greedo. In the original version Han Solo was the only one to shoot, but in the re-release, the scene had been altered to make it look as if Han Solo shot only after Greedo shot first. Many people find such tinkering unacceptable, and this is the kind of stuff that parents sharing pop culture passions with their children discuss in great detail.

The movie *E.T. the Extra-Terrestrial* was similarly doctored for its twentieth anniversary re-release to replace guns in the hands of police with walkie-talkies.

Fun fact: Fans don't like their films messed with, not even by the director.

"I Am the Walrus" is a song written by John Lennon and performed by the Beatles that has sparked much discussion over the years. There are various theories about what the rather whimsical and nonsensical lyrics mean.

Kids love music, and they love seeing their parents passionate about something they (the parents) enjoy. Bonding over bands, pondering lyrics, and dancing around in the living room are just some of the wonderful moments that a catchy tune can inspire.

Dance with your kids, people!

The World Within

Some people are always running with the crowd, whether they are leading it or clinging tightly to its shirttails, and kids are no different. In many cases, there is an innate desire to be a part of something bigger, and that something bigger is playing the newest games, wearing the coolest shoes, and seeing movies that are entirely inappropriate. They say it is good to play well with others.

Parents are often concerned about children who choose their own company over that of others. A child's preference for solitude is often misconstrued as social awkwardness. Some parents worry that it implies "dangerous" loner tendencies. Granted, both points may be valid, and parents should not ignore such signs. But generally speaking, a child who enjoys his own company over that of the masses is probably a great kid to be around. The important thing is not to stigmatize the kid but rather, to engage in enough interaction to get a sense of the reasons for that preference.

TYPICAL PHRASE YOU MIGHT HEAR: *I don't want to play with them.*

VARIATIONS: *I don't like what they're playing. That game doesn't interest me.*

This is okay. If the child has a relatively healthy sense of self-esteem and an endless imagination, then occasional time alone may be the perfect opportunity to expand both.

WHAT TO SAY: *What do you want to play?*

VARIATION: *What does interest you?*

Getting a little insight into why the child wants to play alone, or what it is he plans to do with his time, should put your mind at ease. It is also a great time to let your child share his imagination aloud to an actual audience—this is an opportunity to reaffirm the child's belief in his creative process.

WHAT NOT TO SAY: *If you play by yourself, the other kids will think you're weird.*

VARIATIONS: *Don't give the other kids a reason to think you're a misfit/freak/loser.*

Yes, people actually say such things to their children. This is a terrible blow to a child's self-worth and can result in doubts and anxieties that lead to serious issues.

There is nothing wrong with encouraging a child to play with other kids—but there is no reason to badger him into it. Support what he wants to do, and he'll do it with confidence.

THE LONE WOLF IS SHY AND CORNERED

While many children decline invitations to play with others for the reasons we have touched upon, it is not uncommon for other factors to be at work. Children may refuse the company of others because of abnormal shyness or insecurity. Such traits may be the result of previous experiences that include, but are not limited to, the child being teased, bullied, or made to feel embarrassed for one reason or another.

Such abusive peer behavior may have been meant in jest, but the child who is suffering is not interested in the intentions of the abusers. He just wants a safe playing environment, and playing alone is the best way for him to ensure it.

If you suspect your child is avoiding other children out of fear or as the result of unkind treatment, you should discuss the matter with the child and seek professional help as needed.

There is nothing wrong with playing alone, but it should be a choice made freely, not out of worry.

Tales of a Playground Loner

"What do you do at recess?" Anne asked her sons.

The six-year-old rambled off a list of activities and games that seemed rather extensive for a handful of twenty-minute increments, but apparently he believes in seizing the day.

"Nothing," said the nine-year-old, without a hint of melancholy. It was just an answer, matter-of-fact, and heartbreakingly honest.

"You must do something," Anne said.

"Yesterday I looked for my friend, and I finally found him and some other kids in the far restroom. They were hiding behind the trashcan and playing on their phones."

"What did you do?"

"They were being sneaky. We aren't supposed to have phones, so I left."

"Good. What about your other friends?" Anne asked, listing each of them one by one.

"He always plays handball," her son said. "He always plays . . ." and he responded to each name with an activity that didn't interest him.

"It seems to me," Anne offered, "and this is just a suggestion, but perhaps you should spend your time doing things you like rather than looking for other people. Go to the thing you enjoy, or make up your own game to play. You have friends everywhere."

He nodded thoughtfully.

"When I got tired of looking around, I lay beneath the big shade tree."

"You lay there?" his mother asked. "Doing what?"

"Resting," he said, "and thinking."

Everyone was quiet for a spell, each gazing in the direction of her or his choosing.

"Did you know that there is a door at the bottom of the big shade tree?" he asked. His brother perked up.

"It's not a real door," he continued, apparently concerned that they were *too* intrigued. "It looks like a real door, but it is small."

"Did you open it?" asked his brother.

"Even if it was a real door I wouldn't know how to open it," he said, and then he looked back toward that faraway place.

"What do you think lives there?" Anne asked.

"I don't know," he answered. "I'm more curious about where it goes."

"Any ideas?" Anne asked.

"I suppose," he said, "that it could go just about anywhere."

And then Anne stopped worrying about how he spends his recess.

Teamwork in Progress

While solitude has its merits, there are plenty of positive reasons for children to play together. For example, it helps to develop a sense of belonging to something bigger than themselves—to be a part of a team. After all, teamwork wins championships (and other things). It is important for kids to learn to trust others and, in turn, to be trusted by them. There is no "I" in team, but it also doesn't work unless everyone does his or her part, and that takes effort.

TYPICAL PHRASE YOU MAY HEAR: *Why can't I just do what I want to do?*

VARIATION: *I can do it by myself.*

Working and/or playing as part of a team might take a bit of adjustment. The transition between doing what the child wants to do and doing what is best for the group can be a rocky one, but the rewards are great, and kids generally come to appreciate the camaraderie and overall sense of accomplishment that results from reaching goals together. It is good to be counted on, and it is good to know that one is worthy of the confidence of others.

WHAT TO SAY: *If everyone did what only they wanted, then nothing would get done.*

VARIATION: *Sometimes you need the help of others, and they, in turn, need you.*

The easy example here is sports, but teamwork is not limited to that arena. There are academic projects, extracurricular organizations, religious groups, and many other contexts where teamwork is both fun and vital—not to mention laying the groundwork for being a contributing member of society. However, the best example of teamwork in action is family.

WHAT NOT TO SAY: *You are the best one on the team.*

VARIATION: *You don't have to listen to anyone else.*

There may be times when these statements are actually positive reinforcement for a child, but in this example of encouraging teamwork, they serve only to undermine the benefits of group play. In order for a child to function successfully within a team, she must accept the fact that, win or lose, they are all in it together.

Free Adventure Time!

At some point parents started to fear unstructured play—at least many of them are convinced that every moment of a child's life needs to be scheduled. Kids can't just goof off all summer doing what they want to do. They have to go to camp all day and straight to soccer practice when it's over. Twice on Saturdays.

Free time and unstructured play are the enemy of the leisure police. And I'm here to tell you that they're dead wrong. Sure, structure has its place, but to believe that a child needs every moment accounted for is doing him a great injustice. He needs downtime, and he needs time to explore who he is and what he likes to do. He needs an opportunity to create his own schedule.

TYPICAL PHRASE YOU MAY HEAR: *I'm going on an adventure.*

VARIATION: *Do you want to play a game I made up?*

This is childhood. Look at it closely. It is beautiful.

It is during free time that children are most likely to develop the creativity and ingenuity that shape their perception of the world and how they fit in it. This is where they practice problem solving and learn to apply skills that will benefit them in more structured settings.

Note that the idea of free time does not mean that the child has to play by himself—it also makes for great unstructured group play.

WHAT TO SAY: *Let's pack you a snack and some water. Do you have a map?*

VARIATION: *Yes! Of course I do.*

In the first response we are encouraging the child to explore and be imaginative, but also responsible and safe (packing properly). As a bonus, if the adventure makes you a bit nervous, then having the kid create a map to follow is a great way to feed his creativity while making sure, through subtle suggestion, that you know where his adventure leads.

As for joining in playing the game he has created, you probably need that even more than he does.

WHAT NOT TO SAY: *Adventures are dangerous.*

VARIATION: *I don't have time to play.*

Most children aren't looking for danger, they are looking for excitement—there is a difference. By playing with your child, you take a big step toward controlling any danger and turning it into excitement. If you are really concerned about safety, then appoint yourself the safari guide, pack a snack, and get the map ready. You are going on an adventure!

In regard to time, this is a sensitive issue. We have demands on our time that children cannot comprehend, and sometimes, because of those demands, we have to disappoint our offspring. But at the end of the day, or during most any other interval when the opportunity arises, allowing fifteen minutes for playtime with your child is going to mean a lot more than adjusting the font on your report (Comic Sans is fine).

It's How You Play the Game

Teaching kids to play games can be an exercise in frustration. Children love to play games, but they don't necessarily like to play them in the way that the game designers intended. This is fine to an extent, but at some point they need to play right or it isn't fun for anyone.

There is a fine line between creative interpretation of the rules and blatant disregard for them. If you need further proof, let your kid be the banker in Monopoly—Wall Street, take note. On the one hand we are all about encouraging their imagination, but on the other we want to make sure that they don't develop a habit of cheating.

Read the rules together. Talk about them. Ask each other questions, and prepare yourself for the hypotheticals.

TYPICAL PHRASE YOU MAY HEAR: *I wasn't on that space. I started on this one.*

VARIATIONS: *You messed up my turn, so I get to go again. I don't want to follow that rule. That's a stupid rule.*

This is a teaching moment, where teaching does *not* consist of your tossing the game board across the room and declaring that the fun is over (as tempting as that may be). Take a breath.

WHAT TO SAY: *You need to play fair, just like the rest of us.*

VARIATIONS: *If you win a game by not playing fair, then you aren't really winning. The same rules apply to everyone.*

Boom. Knowledge dropped.

Playing upon a child's desire to win can be tricky in its own right; you don't want to create a culture where winning is the only acceptable outcome. There is nothing wrong with losing a game—winning is just more fun. However, the child's desire to win is a great ally in enforcing fair and honest play. Winning isn't winning if the gameplay was dishonest.

The flip side is that you need to be quick with "Good game!" and "That was a lot of fun!" if their fair play results in a loss. Let them know how much you appreciated their time, effort, and company. Playing board games as a family is about doing something fun together, not beating and taunting people you care about.

WHAT NOT TO SAY: *Cheater!*

VARIATION: *You are ruining the game for the rest of us!*

Relax. You are trying to teach a lesson, not break their spirit. The object is to show the child that his disregard for the rules of the game is making it unpleasant for the other players and may lead to a time when nobody wants to play with him—but without saying it quite that bluntly. Let him know that you won't play again if he doesn't play right, but give him every opportunity to correct his behavior without the argument escalating into something more. After all, it's just a game.

CHAPTER 5

Family Feuds
and Fun Time

There is nothing like family, whether they are sharing your laughter or pushing your buttons with red-hot pokers. They understand you and claim you anyway, which is very reassuring for both kids and adults.

Lately there has been a popular theory suggesting that in the United States, the emphasis on family has been greatly reduced over recent generations. People cite that decline as the cause of whatever they say is Wrong With This Country. They might be right.

There are more benefits to having a strong, supportive family than to going it on one's own. Even though that principle is quite obvious, we sometimes have trouble putting it into practice.

However you define your family, from the smallest group to the largest, the key ingredient is love. Regardless of loss or distance, that is the one thing that never changes. No child has ever been loved too much. And no adult, for that matter.

Forget the arguments and conflicts that may arise—that's just someone caring about you no matter what and making sure you know it. Respect that, and return the favor.

Family comes first, and the more we remember that, the happier we will be.

This chapter is about enjoying family to the fullest, even when they are pushing those buttons.

Who's on First?

First is big with kids. Even more so than it is with sports commentators. Being first means winning and raking in the spoils. It establishes perceived (or actual) pecking orders, lists, and rankings.

First matters. And in the world of childhood, it matters a lot.

TYPICAL PHRASE YOU MAY HEAR: *I had it first!*

VARIATIONS: *I go first. I was first.*

This is the ultimate phrase that children love to use when establishing ownership of the object(s) of their choice. Such an object can be a toy, a TV remote, or a tube of toothpaste. The "it" is inconsequential, and everybody knows it.

However, "ownership" itself is among the most important things to a child, as is clearly evident in the exclamation mark that resounds whenever that phrase is spoken. Ownership, in the parlance of childhood, is most often defined by establishing that siblings have no legitimate claim (or hands) on the disputed item. Ever.

Note: Having it first, much like a pinky swear, does not expire. Ownership can be relinquished only by the goodwill of the child, the firm line of adult authority, or the gradual fading of time until all things have passed to dust. The latter is, by far, the easiest option.

The first (see, it *is* important!) thing for you to do is assess the situation, identify the object in question, and hear every side of the story to establish rightful ownership, if any. Don't take this lightly. Your response will depend on the seriousness of the facts with regard to the object, the repercussions of official proprietorship, and the presence of tears and/or blood.

WHAT TO SAY: *It's not a race.*

VARIATIONS: *It doesn't matter who had it first. It belongs to all of us/doesn't belong to anyone.*

Acquaint yourself with this phrase because you will see it again. In fact, you may want to put this one on speed dial. The main point is to let the child know that the item in question is, in most cases, not going anywhere. There is plenty to go around, and there is no reason to rub it in everybody's face. That's just not cool.

This is also a great opportunity to discuss sharing, taking turns, being considerate of others, and all of the other golden rules that parents love so much (rightfully so). Basically, this is when you reward generosity and kindness, rather than punishing any moments of self-serving eagerness. Kids love to rise to the occasion, and it is our job as parents to give them every chance to do so.

WHAT NOT TO SAY: *If you don't share, you can't play with it/use it at all.*

VARIATIONS: *If you can't share, nobody gets to play with it.*

By denying the child time with the object, you're encouraging the idea that ownership is some sort of primal need. At the next opportunity, he'll try all the harder to be first with the object. He may even consider breaking other family rules in order to enjoy the item (that is, sneaking). History has shown that people want what they cannot have, and they will go to great lengths to get it—kids are no different.

Sibling Rivalry

There is a reason why civil wars are especially painful. (Not that any war is a bed of roses, except, of course, the actual Wars of the Roses. But I digress.) A civil war is especially painful because it literally pits sibling against sibling. There are no winners here.

Obviously, sibling rivalry isn't the same as a civil war, but on a smaller, more intimate scale, it can be pretty upsetting to watch—especially for the parents of those involved. Plus, you have to get two separate uniforms. It's all so time-consuming.

Luckily, most sibling rivalry is based more on heated competition than on acts of war, although you wouldn't know it from the level of insults being traded. Each just wants to beat the other. There can be only one winner.

TYPICAL PHRASE YOU MAY HEAR: *I'm better than you.*

VARIATION: *You suck.*

Some kids compete in order to showcase their superiority, while others aim to prove that their siblings aren't as good— there is a difference. Frankly, the latter just seems mean.

You can't do much to check their competitive spirit (and you shouldn't), but you can do your best to downplay the importance of winning. Yes, this might go against the grain for many people, but is there really any benefit in acknowledging one child as better than the others? These things are contagious and can spill over into other parts of the sibling relationship.

It is fine to praise something special that one child has achieved; in fact, she should be lauded. But you and she don't need to celebrate by putting down another kid.

WHAT TO SAY: *Doing something better doesn't mean you are a better person.*

VARIATIONS: *You both did a great job. I'm proud of both of you.*

That'll larn 'em. The reply is common sense, but it needs to be reiterated from time to time. Besting someone in competition does not mean bettering him or her in life. You can point out that different people have different skill sets and leave it at that.

WHAT NOT TO SAY: *You aren't as good as your brother.*

VARIATION: *Your sister is better than you.*

Nobody casts a shadow like a successful sibling, and even though his or her accomplishments are something to be celebrated, they should not evoke negative comparisons with others. That isn't fair to anyone and can lead to resentment between children when there should be nothing but pride and support.

WINNER, WINNER, CHICKEN DINNER

As competitive as siblings might be, and as strongly as each may want to best the other, their competitiveness often escalates when they unite against foes from outside the family. Seriously, the only thing harder than playing against a super-competitive person is playing against such a person and her or his siblings (see *The Brady Bunch*).

Good luck with that.

Sibling Bonds

Whether or not kids with siblings are willing to admit it, they have no better friends in their corner than each other. They have each other's backs, and they are united against such foes as bedtimes, bullies, and broccoli.

Siblings who get along well are about the sweetest thing a parent could ask for—especially if they are getting along well in the other room when *Game of Thrones* is on television. Everybody wins.

The closeness of siblings, whether they are a dynamic duo or deep enough to field their own soccer team, may make them role models for each other, confidants, and partners in crime (where "crime," we trust, equals good-natured shenanigans). There are sure to be disagreements and tears, but no bond could be tighter.

Many of the phrases that commonly arise during interactions between siblings, regardless of how close they are to one another, will be discussed in other parts of this book. Here I'll talk about a situation wherein the bond is broken, albeit temporarily.

TYPICAL PHRASE YOU MAY HEAR: *Why can't I go with _____?*

VARIATIONS: *I don't want to stay by myself. Why don't they want me to go?*

It might be a week at camp, a friend's birthday party, or any number of other situations in which one sibling requires time without the other(s). Whatever the occasion, the kids are separated, and one feels very left out.

WHAT TO SAY: *This is a great opportunity for you, too!*

VARIATION: *Why don't you take advantage of this time?*

The glass is half full. Don't let anyone tell you otherwise.

The child left behind (that sounds way too ominous) must have *something* she likes to do that is routinely hindered by the presence of others—frame the current situation as a chance to do it! Now try it with a little enthusiasm.

Of course, if you choose to spin this time as a special moment for you and the child to hang out together, which is a wonderful idea, be prepared to offer that same opportunity for attention when the other child is home alone with you. Special moments in a busy home are the high-stakes jackpot of lifelong memories. Again, everybody wins.

WHAT NOT TO SAY: *It's not you. It's them.*

VARIATIONS: *They don't want you to go. They want to do something without you.*

Look, this isn't the Denny's parking lot on the way home from my senior prom—nobody is breaking off a relationship here. This is just about people (kids are people, too!) needing a bit of time to do their own thing.

Going out on their own (without siblings, not necessarily without supervision) allows children to create their own space and their own identity. It is a chance to grow. Time apart is healthy for any relationship. However, if we suggest *it's them*, meaning that the child's siblings have chosen to desert her, then we are planting the potential seeds of animus or anxiety where none exist. In the process we hammer home the fear that she was excluded for a reason.

She and her sibling(s) will all be back together soon enough, and then there will be new stories to tell, which is nice.

Everybody is still winning in this one.

When Stuffed Animals Die

He stood at the top of the stairs and waited for me to notice him. He held a tiny arm in his, making his own appear massive by comparison. One end of the tiny arm was a gloved hand frozen in an eternal wave. The other end was torn and littered with fluff. He stood at the top of the stairs and he didn't say a word.

"Is it Mickey?" I asked. He nodded that it was.

"It's his," he said. His younger brother was downstairs doing his homework and eating his fill of little fish crackers.

"He doesn't know," he added. "The dogs did it. I found it in the bedroom."

The dogs hadn't chewed anything they shouldn't in years, but the past few weeks had found them inside the house more often than not, and they had grown bored and weary. The various stuffed animals of the boys had become a means to burn energy and take out frustrations. At first it was a random rabbit here, a gruff old gorilla there—the fringes of a stuffed animal collection grown to an awkward abundance, and even though I knew the dogs were in the wrong, I was silently thankful for their natural thinning of the herd.

The boys took to placing their fiber-filled friends under beds, stuffing them in closets, and hiding them behind doors that only thumbs could open. Then, when days passed with toys left unmolested, the closets became careless, the doors a little less shut, and through a house cold and empty the dogs would hunt.

There is a hierarchy to all things, and the stuffed toys of a little boy are no different. There are levels of love and shades of "real" that we have all known and most have forgotten, but a handful of mouse held tight against the chest hears the last goodnight from day-worn lips, keeps time with the beat of a heart warm and sleeping, and greets the day with sweet embrace. That is the real of a favorite toy, and to a little boy with sleep in his eyes, it is a real that lasts for always.

The older boy and I walked down the stairs. I held his hand in mine, and he held the glove in his other. We found his brother mid-smile, with a ray of sunshine across his face and his hair a golden tussle. I held the moment as long as I could, willing the story to end on this page, but my older son is one of duty and honor, and where I would hide in the bask of a sun-kissed boy until the sky was shades of fading pinks, orange, and purple, he did the thing he felt he must. There was an exchange from one brother to the other, and then the sun set suddenly beneath the weight of tears.

We have lost loved ones throughout the years, and learned from pets the concept of passing, and while a stuffed mouse may not belong in the same line as those that meant so much, the happiness he brought deserves to be acknowledged. He was the toy we would have kept forever.

My son stood crying, his face buried against my leg, each hand full of pieces that would never go back together, a plush puzzle with parts forever missing. Then there was a soft tapping upon his shoulder, and when he turned he saw the face of a memory, and behind it that of his brother.

"But he's your Mickey," whispered the youngest.

"You can hold him for a while," replied the other. He handed his favorite toy to his only brother, and then my boys stood in the kitchen and they hugged one another, tiny arms around tiny arms and a mouse tight between them with a smile that never wavered, and it never would.

Religion and Politics

They say that religion and politics are topics that should never be discussed in polite company, but who wants to hang out with polite company? There is nothing like a little forceful argument to get the kids interested. Besides, if you don't express your beliefs and views in front of your children, how are they supposed to know what you stand for? Kids enjoy a bit of passionate debate (but they don't care for anger, so make sure they are clear on the distinction).

The key to offering views, thoughts, and theories on matters as widely contested as religion and politics—especially if you are making the case for your child to adopt a similar outlook—is to avoid blanket statements and unnecessary judgment of others.

TYPICAL PHRASE YOU MAY HEAR: *Is God real?*

VARIATION: *Who are you going to vote for?*

VARIATIONS: *What is our religion? Why are we the religion that we are? Why do you vote the way you do? Why do you think some politicians are wrong?*

The answers to these questions are about as personal and honest as anything could ever be. However, others have differing opinions, even though we may not agree with them. This is the time to make your case, not to criticize others. The kids are listening to you, and while most parents hope their kids will share their belief system and political outlook as they get older, there is no guarantee that this will happen. Don't burn bridges before they are built. Furthermore, intolerance is not a good life lesson.

WHAT TO SAY: *This is what I believe . . .*

State your beliefs, and explain why you hold them. If other people in your child's life (spouse, grandparents, etc.) have different viewpoints, give them the same opportunity to share their views. Or at least explain that others believe differently, and provide clear and respectful reasons why that is the case. It is easier than it sounds.

WHAT NOT TO SAY: *What we believe is right, and what they believe is wrong.*

VARIATION: *Don't listen to them.*

Teaching children that it's wrong to engage in debate or respectfully listen to all sides is doing them a terrible injustice. They should agree with your views, not because you say so, but because they believe these things, too. Showering others with vitriol is never a good thing. In some cases it will have the exact opposite result from the one intended. (Many people in the 1960s became political radicals precisely because their parents held conservative beliefs and expressed them frequently.)

The bottom line on politics and religion is that people are going to disagree. Finding ways to work together despite our differences makes all of us stronger. Talk about it to your kids.

Where the Magic Things Are

The merry old land of make-believe is a crowded place, and depending on how you view aliens, the supernatural, or religion it has some pretty interesting inhabitants. Kids grow up believing that various mythical creatures are actually real, no matter how far-fetched their apparent existence. Many of us think this is charming and sweet and would no sooner spoil the innocence for a child than pull the wings off a butterfly. Other parents, though, want nothing to do with the charade.

TYPICAL PHRASE YOU MAY HEAR: *Is the tooth fairy real?*

VARIATION: *Are ghosts real?*

This isn't as black and white as you might think. Although most adults do not believe in the tooth fairy, there are plenty who believe in ghosts—or at least in some kinds of supernatural phenomena. The same can be said for aliens, deities, and Bigfoot. Some folks believe such things are the stuff of stories; others are wholeheartedly convinced of their existence. To each his or her own.

WHAT TO SAY: *Do you believe in fairies?*

VARIATION: *What do you think?*

Chances are that if you are having this conversation with your children, you have encouraged their belief in such magical things. The idea of their expressing doubt probably fills you with a sense of sudden melancholy.

Watching children grow up is terribly bittersweet.

WHAT NOT TO SAY: *Yes.*

VARIATION: *No.*

When dealing with the unexplainable, it is hard to talk in absolutes. You may have your beliefs, but few of us have tangible answers. If your child is starting to express disbelief, then giving a firm reply for *or* against may either uncomfortably accelerate the evolution of his thinking or create a situation where he believes his parent to be a liar. These talks are too delicate for yes or no. You need a more extended discussion that comes to a nuanced conclusion.

As for the things that go bump in the night, many educated people put great stock in the unknown—and do you *really* know the answer? For that matter, do you really *want* to know?

The wildcard in these scenarios is third-party influence and interference. For instance, in nearly every Christmas show, there's a character who doesn't believe in Santa. Usually, of course, the skeptic is proved wrong. However, doesn't the mere introduction of such an attitude suggest that doubt is possible? This is where the questions start.

Peers also contribute their two cents to the conversation, and while their views and experiences may vary, they will almost always add something that you wish they wouldn't. That's kind of their thing.

YES, THERE IS A SANTA CLAUS

In 1897 a little girl named Virginia O'Hanlon asked her father whether Santa Claus was real. Her dad suggested that she write the *New York*

Sun, a prominent newspaper of the time. He told her, "If you see it in the *Sun*, it's so."

The letter was answered by editor Francis Pharcellus Church, a veteran correspondent during the American Civil War, who had never had any children of his own, and whose brother owned the *Sun*. His moving response to the question about Santa's existence, commonly referred to as "Yes, Virginia, there is a Santa Claus," is still popular today.

The reason why the piece remains so engrained in American culture is mainly the logical appeal that Francis Pharcellus Church makes to the child's innocence and imagination. His points are so sound and wonderfully delivered that generations of children and adults alike have kept their belief in Santa Claus, despite those who believe otherwise (and despite the fact that practically no one still thinks we can believe everything we read in a newspaper).

Oh, the Chores

A funny thing about kids is that they love to help. They really enjoy it. Whenever parents need a hand, most kids are quick to offer whatever help they can—even when their help actually makes the project harder or messier for us. We always let them do it. Why? Because they take such pride and pleasure in it that it would be a shame not to let them participate.

However, children do not feel nearly as enthusiastic about chores. They should—after all, chores are just jobs that the kids can do around the house to help their parents out. They should be pleased as punch when we give them the opportunity.

They disagree.

TYPICAL PHRASE YOU MAY HEAR: *I don't want to clean my room!*

VARIATION: *I don't want to take the trash out!*

Most of the conversations surrounding chores consist of parents telling kids to do them and the children whining about it. Every. Single. Time.

There are a number of ways to deal with their response. We can be firm and demanding. We can be soft and let them shirk their responsibilities. We can give them other options that they claim to like better. (I'll give you fair warning: They will be just as adamant against their new chore within a day or two. Give it time.) If we are *real* gluttons for punishment, we can try to reason with them.

WHAT TO SAY: *Everybody in this family does their part to make the house run smoothly. Those chores are your part.*

VARIATION: *When you do your chores, you are being a big help.*

The idea behind reasoning with the child, assuming she is open to such concepts as logic and common sense, is that she will see the difference that her actions make and understand that she is appreciated for doing them. She'll know that she is helping. Tell her "thank you" a lot.

WHAT NOT TO SAY: *As long as you are living under my roof, you will do as I say.*

VARIATION: *Earn your keep.*

These are common phrases that parents tend to throw out in moments of frustration, and they aren't very nice. There's an implied ultimatum: If you don't play by my rules, you can't live here.

First of all, it is a home, not a military school. Discipline is necessary, but it's not rigid, and violating it doesn't result in expulsion. Second, there is no reason to give your child ultimatums that you have no intention of enforcing—either she will call your bluff and lessen your authority, or you will have to actually kick your child out of the house for not cleaning her bedroom, and that is just ridiculous.

The best approach to kids who resist the responsibility of chores is, first, to show them how easy the chores really are compared to other unattractive options and, second, to make the completion of chores a prerequisite to some activities that the kids enjoy.

They may not ever like their chores, but they will do them.

INCENTIVE!

It's easy to create an incentive for kids to complete their chores. For example, they cannot play video games, go to a friend's place, or have the daily Wi-Fi password (this requires you to change it every morning) until their chores are done (and done right). However, when presenting this to them, phrase it in a positive way: "You can go to _____'s house as soon as you've finished _____."

Some children might respond to gold stars on a chart. The stars, one for each completed task, build toward an agreed-upon treat.

Basically, find what they love and hold it hostage—just don't call it that. Ever.

Allowance: Kid, Can You Spare a Dime?

Speaking of chores, have you considered an allowance? As kids start to understand the power of the almighty dollar, they become more inclined to take their rewards in the form of cold, hard cash. This can be a good thing.

TYPICAL PHRASE YOU MAY HEAR: *I need money to buy a new game.*

VARIATION: *I want this toy.*

The wonderful thing about an allowance is that it is *their* money. But it isn't something they get for free; it's money they earn by completing chores. By earning their own money and applying it toward the purchases of their choice, kids gain a better understanding of what a dollar is really worth, and perhaps become a bit more appreciative of the things we buy for them.

WHAT TO SAY: *Save your allowance.*

VARIATION: *Now you have something to work toward!*

He may not like your answer, but it will inspire him to work harder toward his goal—or at least to re-evaluate the item that he wants.

The lessons of working for a dollar and saving money for the things they want will help kids avoid the pitfalls of debt and careless spending as they get older. That, in turn, should help keep you from paying their allowance well into their forties.

WHAT NOT TO SAY: *I don't buy you things anymore; you have your own money.*

The problem with telling a child that all of his wants and desires are now his own responsibility is that it may not reinforce his work ethic. Instead it can create a real disconnect within the system—he just wants a little extra cash, not to strike out on his own. If earning an allowance means no more treats from the parents, then children may not be inclined to participate in the process.

Also, kids don't want to feel as grown up as all that—at least, not yet. They may like the chance to earn some money, but they aren't ready to step into the workforce, and nobody should respect that more than parents. Kids grow up fast enough. They don't need to be unnecessarily rushed.

One other thing to determine when implementing an allowance is how much money is fair and reasonable. We are talking about young children, so their financial needs are modest—nothing on the order of rent, food, and car insurance. However, they do believe their wants to be of great importance. This is not the time to argue perspective. It is time to provide it.

TYPICAL PHRASE YOU MAY HEAR: *I want a raise.*

VARIATION: *Can I get an advance on my allowance?*

Congratulations, your kid is now smarter than you. Best of luck.

The Talk

You don't want to have this conversation. Your kids don't want to have this conversation.

You need to have this conversation.

Talking to kids about sexuality and the reproductive process is important. Obviously, you are concerned about experimentation (it starts younger and younger), which may lead to pregnancies and disease, but there is more to it than that.

Talking to kids about the changes that their bodies will soon face enables them to prepare for the transformation and to accept the normalcy of something that feels anything but. Puberty is on the horizon, and there is some wacky stuff happening there.

TYPICAL PHRASE YOU MAY HEAR: *Where do babies come from?*

VARIATION: *What is sex?*

You may be able to stall with cabbage patches and stork stories for a few years, but the inevitable is out there, and it is fast approaching. Brace yourself.

WHAT TO SAY: *Babies grow in women's bellies.*

VARIATION: *Sex is something for grownups who love each other.*

Digress as needed. Some kids will be ready for more detail than others. Some will relate better to personal stories about their own family, and others may appreciate a more generalized, scientific approach. Teach what they can learn.

In addition to being comfortable with their own development, children need to respect that of others. Everybody is going through some variation of the same thing, but the speed at which it happens, and the visible results, will be unique to each child. It is hard enough without the open mocking and gawking of other children.

TYPICAL PHRASE YOU MAY HEAR: *Some of the kids are starting to change and I am not.*

VARIATION: *I'm the only one changing!*

As much as we want our kids to embrace their individualism and differences, this is something of an exception. Of course, there is nothing wrong with the process happening at different rates with different people. Above all, this is a time for reassurances and understanding. Children in these situations may feel vulnerable and awkward, and our role is to be the voice of reason.

WHAT TO SAY: *Everybody changes at a different rate and in different ways.*

VARIATION: *Everyone has their own clock, and your body is working right on time.*

Something else to consider when preparing for "the talk" with your child is not to let the "the" part of it intimidate you. There is no reason that it all has to take place in one session. It is perfectly acceptable—perhaps even beneficial—to introduce topics and situations in briefer conversations as you see fit. We all want our children to face life as well prepared as possible, but there is no reason to hasten the process. If your relationship is open and close, you will know when certain topics need to be discussed.

WHAT NOT TO SAY: *That is your personal business.*

VARIATIONS: *You aren't ready for this conversation.*

If a child cannot talk to his or her own parent about their personal business, then who can he or she turn to? Denying children access to your experience and love is shutting a door, and they will find others to open—doors you will have no control over.

Parents may feel that a child isn't ready for a conversation of such magnitude, but the reality is if the child has questions he will search for an answer until he gets it. That answer should come from his parents. Perhaps it's not the kid who isn't ready.

Talking about *The* Talk

He was bundled in a coat much too warm for the moment and was carrying a hefty binder with a thick strap over his thin left shoulder. He wore a backpack for overflow on the other.

Normally his father had to pry the occurrences of the day from him, piecing together a timeline from the reluctant account of a potential politician already adept at avoidance and plausible deniability. Conversation during a typical walk to the park went something like this:

"What did you do today?"

From the eight-year-old: "I don't know."

"Did you go to the computer lab?"

"I can't remember."

"Should we stop for some ice cream?"

"Yes!"

All the while, his six-year-old brother provided the color commentary in the pauses between, bouncing around them like a cartoon version of himself drawn slightly off scale:

"What did you do today?"

"I don't know."

"He played dodgeball! I saw his class on the play-ground. They always play dodgeball!"

"Did you go to the computer lab?"

"I can't remember."

"He had library today! I had computer lab! He always has library on the days that I have computer lab! I saw his class in the hall!"

"Should we stop for some ice cream?"

"Yes!"

"Yes!"

But this time was different. Frank stood there wait-ing. His son had the strangest gleam in his eyes. It was distant and heavy and missing some pieces—holes in the blue innocence.

"What do you mean a boy was kicked out of school?" Frank asked, letting his mind run down a list of pos-sible infractions.

"He told another student that he had . . ." He looked around to make sure they were alone. His brother was chasing butterflies, bored with their conversation. "He told another student that he had s-e-x in the shower."

Frank actually hadn't expected that one. His mind raced. "Oh," was the best he could come up with.

"He said he had s-e-x with a girl in the class. He said he had s-e-x in the shower."

"What did the other student do when the kid told him?" Frank asked.

"He told the teacher," his son replied. "And then the boy was kicked out."

"The other student did the right thing," his father told him. They had been spending a lot of time trying to define the difference between reporting bad behavior and being a tattletale. In some cases the fine line is a little bit blurry, but this was not one of them. "That is something you should tell a teacher right away."

They talked more about it. They talked about the little girl and how it must have made her feel to hear someone say such things. They talked about how it was that he had come to hear the sordid details and what the playground consensus was on the matter. They talked about the things people do for attention.

They talked about everything until Frank felt he couldn't avoid the question any longer.

"Do you know what s-e-x is?" he asked.

His son looked around, leaned close, and whispered, "Sex."

"Yes. It's okay to say it. It's not a bad word. Do you know what sex is?"

"No," he admitted. "But you have to be naked."

"Sex is something for grownups," Frank said. "Grownups who care about each other. It's not a bad word, and it is not a bad thing, but it is not for kids. It is for grownups. Grownups who care about each other. Does that make sense?"

"Yes," he said.

"There is going to come a time when we sit down and talk about this more, about sex, and that time is going to be a lot sooner than I care to admit, but you are eight years old, and to be honest, I'm not ready to have that conversation yet . . . unless you are."

The boy's eyes were filling with tears. He leaned into his father's arms and got lost in a hug.

"No," he said. "I don't want to be a grownup yet."

"Okay," Frank whispered, "but if you have any questions I want you to come to me. Don't ever be afraid to come to me. You know that, right?"

"Yes."

He was quiet for a moment, sitting awkward against a cement bench, watching nothing in particular.

"What did you learn?" Frank asked him, unsure of what he'd taught—unsure whether he'd taught anything.

"S-e-x is for grownups that care about each other. It's not bad, but it's not for kids."

He looked his father in the eyes. The man's were tired and heavy, and the boy's blue and sparkling against fading wetness where tears had fallen like a soft spring rain. There was fresh innocence growing in the corners.

"And I can tell you anything," he said.

Frank couldn't see the butterflies. The distance had grown too great. But he could see the space between small feet and cool grass. The sun was brightest there.

"Should we stop for some ice cream?" he asked.

"Yes," he said.

"Then go and get your brother."

PART III

Out and About

CHAPTER 6

School: What Kids Learn and How They Use It

"School days, school days
  Dear old Golden Rule days
  Reading and 'riting and 'rithmetic
  Taught to the tune of the hick'ry stick"
Those lyrics were written in 1907 by Will Cobb and Gus Edwards, and obviously things have changed slightly. For instance, hickory sticks have been replaced by stern e-mails, and there is hardly any dubstep in the entire song, but other than that, school is more or less the same as it was a hundred years ago. Kids walk uphill both ways, they learn stuff, they complain about it, and then they take state-mandated tests to prove their worth to the taxpayers. The Golden Rule days are now.

School may be an institution of learning, but it is much more than that. It is during school that kids examine their own sense of identity, experiment with social interactions, develop relationships, and create dreams. Classroom education is almost secondary to the life lessons our children are learning—just as it was when we were enrolled, but with more computers.

Making the Grade and Citizenship

In earlier sections of this book we covered the idea of charity. Here we're going to cover another aspect of responsible citizenship: behavior.

Actual definitions may vary.

In many school districts in the United States, the term "citizenship" is used to grade children on their attitude, participation, and overall pleasantness. Some kids put more stock in it than others.

TYPICAL PHRASE YOU MAY HEAR: *I got good grades in citizenship because I always listen to the teacher.*

VARIATION: *I got a bad grade in citizenship because I always talk in class.*

There it is. Obviously children need to listen to the teacher, and they should not interrupt in class, but does one type of behavior have more promise than the other?

There is a lot to be said for kindness and being respectful. In fact, those two qualities can take people pretty far in life (assuming that they also have a skill set). Thinking outside the box is promising, too. However, there is no reason to be rude about it.

WHAT TO SAY: *I am so proud of you for getting good grades in citizenship. It is important to be a respectful listener.*

VARIATIONS: *When you are in the classroom, you need to follow the rules. If the teacher says not to talk, then you shouldn't talk. I would love to see you try harder next time.*

Rules are rules, kid. Be kind and respectful to your children, and they will pay it forward. The best thing we can be is a good example.

WHAT NOT TO SAY: *Nobody cares about citizenship.*

VARIATIONS: *Grades don't matter. The teacher is just trying to indoctrinate you.*

This is not being a good example.

The validity of grades is widely debated, but let us assume for the sake of this conversation that good grades are very important. We need to encourage students to do the best they can, no matter what the subject at hand.

Many parents do this by expecting and rewarding good marks. They also balance that by creating negative consequences for poor performance. That generally does the trick, but wouldn't it be great if kids got good grades because they were interested in the subject and had an innate desire to do well? It's just a thought.

TYPICAL PHRASE YOU MAY HEAR: *I got an A in math!*

VARIATION: *I got a D in reading.*

The expectations, rewards, and grade-related punishments that we set for our children should take into consideration their natural aptitude for specific subjects and the amount of effort they put into learning. For instance, isn't a student who struggles with mathematics but worked extremely hard for his C grade at least as worthy of praise as a student who finds math boringly easy and settles for a B?

WHAT TO SAY: *That's fantastic! You worked hard. Let's celebrate!*

VARIATIONS: *It looks like you need to work harder, and I'm here to help you. Let's see if you can get a better grade next time. Why don't you tell me what you're having problems with?*

If you have assigned rewards and penalties to grades in school, then confer those rewards or exact those penalties accordingly, but whether your expectations were exceeded, met, or missed, make sure your child knows how much it means to you for her to try her hardest. Hard work is a great lesson, whatever the grade received.

WHAT NOT TO SAY: *Are you stupid?*

No, she isn't.

The Stars upon Thars

The stars were handed out for one good deed or another. There were kids helping, kids sharing, and kids who just sat quietly. Each star gave its owner a chance to shine brighter, and each child gave each star that he or she earned all the hope that such things warranted.

Children clenched their pencils with gentle fists and scratched their names across the points of paper with anxiety and boldness. The marked stars were then dropped into a small box barely big enough to hold the universe, and they were tossed with exaggerated motion until everyone was satisfied. Then one star was plucked from the cosmos of cardboard, and one smiling child floated toward the prize bin.

No one wins all the time. Winning is a matter of chance, but one's chances increase greatly when one has been awarded many stars based on the actions performed during the week. The stars are earned, etched with names, and pinned to the sky with promise. Then they are boxed, spun, and forgotten in an instant—all but one, and that is when the force of twenty frowns propels one smile upward like a rocket from the carpet. The launch is short and fabulous.

The classroom was filled with parents squeezing into chairs too small and small talk too big for children. It was decorated in early first-grade arts and crafts, and the air was fresh with clean carpet, new paint, and other smells that fade fast beneath the sweet sweat of sun-soaked children. The teacher addressed the adults about the upcoming year, various plans, and the future. The students were nothing but names across the desktops, and parents introduced themselves accordingly.

The teacher explained the concept of stars, how students earned them, and the prize bin that every constellation pointed toward. Then she talked for quite a while about one little boy who had filled his pockets with golden brilliance from acts of kindness, and how she had come to realize that he was taking the stars and sharing them with those who had not earned as many. He thought it only right that those he cared for have their chances matched to his, and in caring for everyone, he boosted their chances considerably.

The woman smiled when she realized the boy in question was her son.

"I earned the stars by being respectful of others," he told her. She had rushed home to tell him how proud she was, and her plans beyond that were just to hold him. He was happy to be mentioned.

"And listening to the teacher," he added.

"I am proud of you," she said. "It is important to be a respectful listener. Why didn't the other kids get stars of their own?"

"Some of them need to try a little harder," he said. "I try to help them."

"That's fantastic," she said. "You worked hard. Let's celebrate."

Stars may be given, taken, or thrown away, and they may twinkle, shoot, or fall, but when stretched forever by small, warm hands, they shine bright on all of us. His smile did that, too.

The Dog Ate My Homework, Again

Homework is the scourge of childhood. It is time-consuming, and much of it is unnecessary busy work, but when well planned, it also helps to reinforce better study skills and overall work ethic. Unfortunately that doesn't seem to happen enough.

Even at its best, homework sends a mixed message, and parents claim to dislike it even more than their children.

Kids in elementary school don't need to spend two hours on a Tuesday night doing homework. That is time best spent with family, which is exactly why parents should assist their kids as needed—it speeds up the process and creates quality time together. Note that there is a difference between *helping* students with their schoolwork and *doing* it for them. The latter doesn't do them any favors.

TYPICAL PHRASE YOU MAY HEAR: *Can you help me with this problem?*

VARIATION: *What's the answer to this problem?*

Granted, it is nice to know your child assumes you have the answers to everything, but the latter request is a perfect example of kids trying to cut corners, whereas the former is an opportunity to instruct. Also, fourth-grade math is hard.

WHAT TO SAY: *Let me see what you have done so far, and we will figure out the next step together.*

VARIATION: *I won't tell you the answer, but I'll show you how to find it for yourself.*

This is where you sit with your child and talk through each step of the process, dissect and dispel any confusion, and show your work. Carry the one.

WHAT NOT SAY: *Here, I'll do it.*

VARIATION: *You are doing it wrong. The answer is X.*

Again, doing the work for a child does not benefit him in any way, although he may argue to the contrary. This problem is just one of many in life, and if he cannot learn to solve problems himself, then he is in for a long struggle. Help him prepare for the future by helping him in the now. Someday he'll thank you for it.

TYPICAL PHRASE YOU MAY HEAR: *I have to read this whole book by Friday.*

Book reports can help or hurt in developing a child's reading skills. Kids are made to read, which can be good, but forcing them to read may build resentment rather than instill a lasting love of literature. This is a great opportunity for you to re-establish your love of the written word and let your kid see you read. Often.

WHAT TO SAY: *Looks like you had better get reading. Let me grab my book, and I'll join you on the couch.*

Now that is quality time.

WHAT NOT TO SAY: *That sounds boring. I bet there's a summary of it on the Internet.*

Are you even paying attention?

Teaching to the Test and Why Everybody Hates It

Ask any parent what she dislikes the most about public education. She'll probably respond that the states exert so much pressure on the schools to ensure that their students achieve certain levels of mastery on mandatory tests that there is no time to teach anything but the subjects covered on those tests. Test results translate into government dollars, and the teachers aren't excited about that either.

The problem with this "teaching to the test" is that education is so much bigger than that. There are so many exciting, interesting, and engaging topics, not to mention fundamental skills, that go neglected because they are not part of the testing. It is incredibly frustrating to know that children are graduating from public schools with holes in their education and backpacks full of untapped potential.

TYPICAL PHRASE YOU MAY HEAR: *We are taking practice tests all week, so I'm supposed to go to bed early.*

VARIATIONS: *We have testing this week, so I'm supposed to eat a good breakfast.*

Really, state-mandated-test administrators? Don't you think that parents try to ensure that their kids get the appropriate amount of sleep and a balanced breakfast *every* day?

Well, most days.

WHAT TO SAY: *Are you ready for the test?*

If they are ready for anything, it is the test. The subjects thereof have been the focus of the entire year, and all they need from you is a few words of encouragement. A hug is a nice touch.

TYPICAL PHRASE YOU MAY HEAR: *That's all I am ready for.*

Touché, kid. Touché.

WHAT NOT TO SAY: *This test is the most important part of the school year.*

They've heard it, and it is our job to make sure they aren't buying it. Yes, testing is important as far as funds, rankings, and all of the stats that benefit the school (and thereby the children) are concerned, but enough with the pressure already. They are kids, not pawns of the system. That said, there's no point in complaining about state-mandated testing in front of your child. It's not as if he can do anything about it. More important, such complaining on your part sends a message that he shouldn't care how he does on the test.

TYPICAL PHRASE YOU MAY HEAR: *The school says that you should quit complaining about the way state testing controls the subject matter taught in classrooms and the restrictions it places on our teachers and our learning potential.*

WHAT TO SAY: *Sorry about that.*

Extracurricular Excitement

Student Council, band, drama, woodshop, football, cheerleading, soccer, swimming, school paper . . . the list of possibilities is endless, and your kid probably wants to join something.

Encourage your kids to be as active as possible. Sure, it will look good on their transcripts someday, but the immediate benefit is fun, challenges, and being a part of something—the transcripts can wait a few years.

TYPICAL PHRASE YOU MAY HEAR: *Can I join track?*

VARIATION: *I want to try out for the school musical.*

Great and great. Getting involved in something bigger than themselves is a fantastic opportunity for kids to practice social skills, gain confidence (and in some cases better health), and develop a sense of belonging. It doesn't matter what it is that they want to do; what matters is that they want to do it.

WHAT TO SAY: *Of course! That is exciting!*

VARIATIONS: *You bet! Do you need any help?*

All they need from you is support and maybe a few bucks for the required uniform. Money might be tight, but support should be easy to find. Share it as often as you possibly can.

WHAT NOT TO SAY: *I don't know. What about the other clubs?*

Chances are that if you are saying something like this to your child, it is because he is interested in something that you are not. Perhaps you had a bad experience with whatever he wants to do, or you don't think he would enjoy it. Don't project your past onto his future. The only way to know whether he will enjoy it is to let him try.

In addition to the benefits just listed, there are plenty of other positive reasons to join extracurricular clubs at school. But are there any negatives?

The biggest hurdle is time. Extra activities require extra time, and that means staying later after school and/or attending events scheduled for the weekend. This will probably necessitate more commitment from you than you honestly expected to give. Welcome to parenting.

TYPICAL PHRASE YOU MAY HEAR: *I have practice at 7 A.M. on Saturday morning.*

VARIATION: *I have a performance at the same time as your big meeting.*

Of course he does.

This is Murphy's Law as it applies to school activities. Whenever a scheduled event *can* cause maximum conflict, it *will*.

Yes, getting up at the crack of dawn on Saturday morning is tough (though worth it), but what do you do about the performance and the meeting?

WHAT TO SAY: *I'll try my hardest to be there.*

Don't make promises you can't keep, but don't make a habit of missing his shows. Meetings aren't going anywhere.

WHAT NOT TO SAY: *My job is more important.*

Is it really?

The Popular Kids

As kids get older, social lines start to form. It is hard to tell who draws them and where or why, but it happens. Suddenly one side is more popular than the other.

It is probably a combination of many factors. Sports, pop culture, family influence, and outward appearance surely play a role in the intangible distinction between the haves and the have nots (or, if you like, between the cool kids and the less cool kids); but so too should good grades, school and community involvement, personality traits, and social endeavors.

Regardless of why kids wind up where they do on the social spectrum, the invisible and fairly meaningless separation that it creates will seem all-powerful and all-important for much of your child's school career. This would be ridiculous if not for the problems such mindsets can cause.

TYPICAL PHRASE YOU MAY HEAR: *She is cool because she's a jock.*

VARIATION: *She gets picked on because she reads comic books.*

Kids like labels as much as the next guy. Unfortunately, pigeonholing children can lead to a lot of angst, sadness, and potential bullying situations.

WHAT TO SAY: *People should not be either picked on or looked up to because of the activities they choose to pursue.*

VARIATIONS: *There is nothing cool about judging others or acting negatively toward them.*

Most of us have been children at one time or another, and whether we want to or not, we can relate to what they are saying. Perhaps you think this is something that doesn't need to be addressed until high school, but that is not the case. Stereotypes emerge early, and kids spend the entirety of their school years falling into them. The holes only get deeper.

WHAT NOT TO SAY: *Just stay away from the jocks. They are jerks.*

VARIATION: *She is a nerd, and everybody knows that nerds get picked on.*

Both of these phrases, whether applied maliciously or just thoughtlessly, justify the "them against us" mentality that permeates many schools. Don't become part of the problem.

To be clear, these extremes of childhood behaviors have practically become clichés, and describing them sounds almost like parody, but they do still exist, and they still cause issues where none need to be.

TURNING THE LABEL TABLE

It is widely believed that the rigid classifications of the tween and teen years, as painful or incredible as they may be, tend to flip once students move into the real world. The classic case is the "nerd" who gets rich and the "jocks" who end up working for her. Although cases can surely be found to support this theory, it remains, for the most part, one more needless stereotype. Encourage your kids to define themselves, not to be defined by others. It may not prove popular, but it should make school a lot more enjoyable.

There is nothing wrong with being a jock, a nerd, or popular. Each kid is an individual and has the ability to control his or her own destiny and actions, but he or she might need some parental support.

We need to be there with answers, advice, understanding, and guidance—and as shoulders to cry on. That is our job, and that is the message we need to send.

WHAT TO SAY: *What matters is how people treat each other.*

VARIATION: *Being cool is the new cool.*

What Makes Kids Popular?

"Oh, she's a really popular kid," said the little girl walking on the sidewalk. The man behind her followed her gaze and wanted to ask why the "she" in question was so popular but decided to see how it played out. His sons just nodded.

Still, he couldn't help but wonder, how do you quantify popularity? Where does popularity come from? When do kids learn how to be popular?

He remembered kids who were popular in elementary school when he was a kid, but many of them peaked early, and by high school they were just members of the pimpled masses. Then there were those who maintained their level of popularity well into the real world, and sometimes, late at night, he could still hear them smiling from some distant hallway.

He had been fairly popular throughout school, but he never met any of the criteria that seemed to be the basis of so many stereotypes. He wasn't a jock, noticeably handsome, or rich. He was just a guy with a sense of humor and great taste in music. He had always believed that people should never be judged on the activities they chose to pursue, but unfortunately not everyone had always agreed.

But that was then, and while those stereotypes still exist (according to TV—he hadn't been a kid in a long time), it had been his personal experience that the rise of geekdom had helped level the playing field between what was once considered popular and what was not. "Nerd" was no longer a label to be stitched into one's wedgie-torn undies, but a badge to be worn with pride. Actual nerds may vary.

His kids were as likely to play soccer as to read a comic book, and he wasn't sure where either path could lead. He made the point that everybody brings something to the table, and cool is as cool does. *There is no us*, he told his kids. *There is no them.*

Elementary school is full of dorky little kids being dorky little kids and loving every minute of it. When do they have time to care about hierarchies and the perception of status? At what point do the pecking order of popularity and the acceptance of social contracts/injustice start? On what are they based?

I'm not even sure that I would want my kids to be popular, he thought. Sure, he wanted them to be liked by their peers and to have good friends, but there are a lot of trappings to popularity that he would rather they not have to deal with. He wouldn't want them to feel like they had to be something that they were not. *I want them to be, first and foremost, comfortable with themselves,* he thought.

That night there was an event for parents at the school where, thanks to two different conversations, he was able to peek behind the curtain of popularity. First, one of the teachers mentioned that she considers his older son a leader. It was news to him. Does being a leader make a kid any more popular than the kids following his lead? Does it matter?

Then he heard that his younger son, according to classmates, is very popular—that everyone wants to be his friend. Did it feel good? Of course, but he wasn't going to let the moment escape without getting to the bottom of the situation.

"Why," he asked, "is he popular?"

"Because he doesn't hit anyone," they said.

That actually made a lot of sense. Apparently being popular *can* be based on how you treat other people. Suddenly, popularity sounded kind of cool.

On Missing School

Schools, for better or worse—and most of us would probably say for worse—are in the business of satisfying the powers that be and attracting funds. They make their money by putting kids in seats and then forcing them to digest the standard curriculum. Should a kid *not* be in her seat for any prolonged period of time, then the school does not get the funding it would otherwise have received. And school administrators don't appreciate that.

To be fair, the schools need money to pay teachers and staff, as well as to buy supplies and the tools of the trade; that is very legit. That is money well spent.

Hence the firm hand governing school absences: Without our kids in class, schools cannot afford to have our kids in class. It's all so circular.

The other important consideration is that kids need to be in school to learn what schools are teaching. After all, you can't learn if you aren't taught. Again with the circles.

But life isn't all book learning.

There are many amazing things to be found via travel, days at work with Mom or Dad, and random afternoons of hooky. In fact, such out-of-the classroom opportunities may be just as important as anything printed in a textbook. These things are worth an absence or two, and don't let anyone tell you otherwise.

TYPICAL PHRASE YOU MAY HEAR: *Can we go to the museum on your day off?*

VARIATION: *Am I allowed to miss school to come on the trip?*

There are sure to be some parents who disagree with those of us who let our kids miss school to attend special events and trips. When all is said and done, how is a perfect attendance record going to compare to a magical adventure?

WHAT TO SAY: *Let's make sure there isn't a big test or special event at school that day, and if there isn't, then we can go!*

VARIATION: *We wouldn't go on the trip without you!*

The good thing about missing school for a trip is that many states allow children to do a project based on the educational value of the experience and present it to the class upon their return. In many cases, if the child misses five consecutive days under this agreement, he or she isn't even marked absent by the school, which consequently retains any funding it would lose otherwise.

WHAT NOT TO SAY: *Your school attendance is more important than our having a special day together.*

VARIATION: *Maybe you can stay at Grandma's house while the rest of us go.*

Nothing is more important than spending a special day with your child. Sure, it may require some planning around soccer games and business meetings, but it should happen as often as possible.

As for going on a family vacation minus a child—you may as well put her travel costs toward therapy now, because that is going to leave a mark. Truth is, while parents need time to themselves, leaving a child home while the rest of you go on a trip that was intended to include him or her feels terrible. That's why they call it a guilt trip.

TAKING HOMEWORK ON VACATION

Obviously you don't want to go out of your way to cause your kid to miss school, but sometimes a family vacation during the school year cannot be passed up. Parents may get their allotted vacation time only during that period, and many family destinations offer amazing discounts in what is considered their off-season. It may be the only vacation opportunity that a family will have, and that time together trumps a week in class that looks just like all the rest.

There are a lot of websites dedicated to the schoolwork options and other school-sanctioned ideas for traveling kids, which range from keeping journals to creating photo essays. Plan the project before you start your vacation, and allow ample time for it to be completed during the trip. Don't spring it on your kid once you get there. That will feel like a trick, and nobody likes that.

Sick Days

Most schools are very clear about the symptoms of illness that warrant keeping a child home, as well as the timeframe during which these symptoms are displayed. Unfortunately, many parents ignore those signs and send their kids to school anyway, disregarding the impact this may have on the healthy kids. Then two days later you feel a tickle in your throat . . . .

TYPICAL PHRASE YOU MAY HEAR: *I have a tummy ache.*

VARIATIONS: *My head hurts. I don't feel good.*

Here is a little secret: Sometimes kids pretend they don't feel well because they don't want to go to school. Seriously, it happens. That being the case, unless you are already privy to the reasons why your child might want to miss school on a given day (tests, bullies, a good book), reserve passing judgment until you've conducted a bit of research.

WHAT TO SAY: *When did you start feeling bad?*

VARIATION: *Have any of your classmates been sick?*

This line of questioning is called "feeling the situation out." You have probably seen something similar on television. It is pretty heady stuff.

Try to find out whether the symptoms your child is complaining about are real, but do so without letting on that you suspect anything. Also, don't call him on his shenanigans until you are sure that he's messing with you. Otherwise, you just look like a big, ol' meanie. The last thing a sick kid needs is a parent who is a big, ol' meanie.

WHAT NOT TO SAY: *You're faking.*

VARIATION: *You're lying.*

You just called your child a fake and a liar, and even if you are right, you probably could have handled it better. Words like "fake" and "liar" tend to leave lasting scars.

TYPICAL PHRASE YOU MAY HEAR: *I threw up.*

VARIATION: *I have diarrhea.*

Call the school, buy some ginger ale, and buckle down for the long haul. There is sickness in the home, and chances are you will get it, too. Take some vitamin C.

WHAT TO SAY: *Get some rest. I will be here if you need me.*

Congratulations! You just pulled first shift. Maybe they'll let you work from home.

WHAT NOT TO SAY: *You are going to school no matter what. I can't miss work.*

You just told your child that he is going to school even if he's actually sick, which is not fair to anyone. You don't like it when other parents send their sick kids to school. Do the right thing.

Thoughts on Teachers

Teaching is one of the most important jobs that anyone can ever have. Unfortunately, those who choose to go into the profession are often not rewarded with a paycheck that reflects that value. This underscores what special people many of those who pursue a career in teaching are, but it hardly seems fair.

A good teacher works with the student, the parents, and the school to ensure that children are taught in a welcoming and safe environment. On top of that, teachers are always furthering their own education, dealing with state and district paperwork, and usually buying classroom supplies out of their own pockets. Teachers are the closest people to superheroes that any of us are likely to meet. The cape is a nice touch.

TYPICAL PHRASE YOU MAY HEAR: *My teacher is making me do yesterday's homework again.*

VARIATION: *My teacher is mean!*

"Mean" in this instance is relative and open to interpretation. On the one hand, we have all had our share of mean teachers (or at least we perceived them as such). It could be that your child is experiencing the same thing. However, it's much more likely that your child's teacher expects a certain level of quality and discipline from a very capable kid who would rather play video games than do homework to the best of her ability. That *is* mean!

WHAT TO SAY: *If you did it right the first time, you wouldn't have to do it again.*

VARIATION: *Your teacher isn't mean. Your teacher wants you to do your best.*

It is easy for parents to get defensive when they think a teacher doesn't understand or care enough about their child— both of which are usually far from the truth. However, when we are getting the story only from an upset six-year-old, it's hard to imagine anything else. Remember, teachers want your child to leave their care and tutelage all the better prepared for the next level of learning and the world around us. They know what they are doing. If you are concerned about something, then speak to them about it. Teachers are a great ally for parents, and vice versa. We are all in this together.

WHAT NOT TO SAY: *Your teacher is wrong.*

VARIATIONS: *Your teacher should not have done that. I can't believe your teacher did that! Don't listen to your teacher.*

Undermining a teacher's authority in order to, theoretically, increase your own on whatever subject or topic is being discussed is not the best way to express any concerns you may have. It pretty much ensures that your offspring will continue to have trouble in that particular class and that the trouble will spread to other classes (since your child now knows that in a conflict between her and her teacher, you'll automatically take her side).

TYPICAL PHRASE YOU MAY HEAR: *My teacher is so cool. We learned a lot today!*

VARIATIONS: *My teacher gave me a sticker for doing a good job!*

These are the words of a kid loving life and enjoying school. That's largely thanks to her teacher. Remember it on Teacher Appreciation Day, but feel free to send a nice card any day of the year.

WHAT TO SAY: *Your teacher is awesome!*

Cooties

Cooties are the stuff of urban legend in its purest form, and they have been scarring children in one form or another for generations. The dictionary defines "cooties" as "a children's term for an imaginary germ or repellent quality transmitted by obnoxious or slovenly people," which would mark the carrier of cooties as something of a schoolyard pariah.

What is special about the spread of cooties is that it seems to respect the boundaries of the playground in terms of contamination—no case of cooties has ever been recorded anywhere except on school grounds.

Sadly, however, the burden of being dubbed a kid with cooties cannot be left in a classroom cubby when the school bell rings. Things like that tend to stay with a child.

TYPICAL PHRASE YOU MAY HEAR: *I don't want to play with them. They have cooties!*

VARIATION: *That kid is gross.*

To be fair, lots of kids are gross, but singling one child out of the yucky masses is not the kindest thing a person can do. You need to make sure your child doesn't become part of a bullying mob.

WHAT TO SAY: *There is no such thing as cooties.*

171

The ugly truth about cooties is that many times, the kid being picked on—and make no mistake, this *is* a form of bullying—may have a characteristic that other children find strange, different, or odd. When this is the case, it is something you need to discuss openly and quickly with your offspring.

It is a sensitive matter, and chances are the children yelling "cooties" have no idea how cruel they are actually being.

WHAT NOT TO SAY: *If you think they are gross, stay away from them.*

Do not miss the opportunity to discuss the many differences between people and to encourage your child to put himself in the "gross" kid's position. How would *he* feel if everybody teased and shunned him for something that was beyond his control? Chances are he wouldn't like it one bit.

Cooties may not be a real condition, but being insensitive toward others is. That malady is very real, but it is something we can cure. Understanding is strong medicine.

TYPICAL PHRASE YOU MAY HEAR: *The kids at school keep saying I have cooties and they won't play with me.*

This is what heartbreak sounds like. There are few things sadder than hearing your child lament the fact that other kids won't play with him—especially over some make-believe silliness spread far and fast.

Speak with the principal and teachers at your child's school. Talk to other parents, and encourage them to address the issue with their own children.

WHAT TO SAY: *They don't know what they are missing.*

Do not let the actions of a few kids make a bigger impact on your child than it already has. Let them know that such things are temporary, and that he is not the one with the problem.

WHAT NOT TO SAY: *Don't be such a baby.*

Just because tough love is an option doesn't mean you need to use it. Your child needs an ally, not another reason to think the kids might be right.

AT LEAST IT'S NOT MY KID . . .

When discussing a group-bullying situation, it is not uncommon for the parents of the perpetrators to express their sincere relief that their child was not the victim of negative attention.

"At least my kid isn't being picked on" seems to comfort them. This is understandable in that no parent wants to see her or his child ridiculed by others. However, these parents seem to forget that the child being picked on is not actually the one with the problem in this scenario. It is their child, and the other children who also participated, who have perpetrated the wrongdoing. There is little comfort to be found in that.

CHAPTER 7

That's What Friends Are For

The relationships that children form over the years are some of the sweetest and funniest bonds they will ever know, and it's pretty awesome to watch them develop. Kids and their friends are the best kind of goofy, and we should encourage them to make the most of it.

Childhood friends share a lot in terms of new experiences, from secrets and confidences to toys, movies, and adventures. The things they explore together will also go far in helping your child discover his or her own interests.

Friends bring out the best in kids and help lay the foundations of trust, respect, and other peer-based qualities that prepare children for adulthood (not that anyone is in a hurry).

Friendship can also have a downside. It is often with friends that kids experience their first arguments, painful betrayals, and the negative effects of peer pressure, which can be blamed for many a bad decision.

When your child makes friends, welcome them and treat them well—after all, your kid is eating cookies at their house, too.

This chapter is about children making friends, the things they do together, the hardships that may arise, and the wonder of it all.

Sleeping Over: The Scare and Care

Sleeping over at a friend's house is a big step in developing self-confidence, and it takes playdates to the next level—a level that stays up way too late playing video games, watching cartoons, and breaking wind as a punch line. It's the good stuff.

It can also be quite terrifying.

TYPICAL PHRASE YOU MAY HEAR: *Can my friend spend the night?*

VARIATION: *Can I stay overnight at my friend's house?*

Throughout recorded history, kids have assumed that planning sleepovers was entirely up to them and required only a courtesy nod for parental involvement. Despite kids' claims to the contrary, you may want to actually speak with the parents of the other child and make sure that everyone is on the same page regarding the pending sleepover.

WHAT TO SAY: *Sure, but I need to talk to [his or her] parents first.*

It's a fairly easy process.

Other parents have the same concerns that you do, namely that the children will be safe, fed, and occasionally supervised. Depending on how well you know the other family, you may want to exchange a bit more information or plan to do something together as a group prior to the sleepover. The point is to put everyone at ease.

Once the sleepover has been scheduled and the moment is nigh, it is important to have one last chat to reiterate every single iota of parenting information and advice that you have implemented over the past several years. *Give or take.* Last-minute reminders are well and good, but stick to the basics.

WHAT TO SAY: *When you are at _____'s house, you are [his or her] guest. Make sure you listen to the parents, follow their rules, eat what they serve you, and use your manners.*

VARIATION: *Pretend we have raised you right and have fun.*

If the child is willing to participate but slightly apprehensive about sleeping away from home and family, make him as comfortable as possible, highlight the potential for endless fun, and leave your phone on.

TYPICAL PHRASE YOU MAY HEAR: *I'm scared.*

We're all scared.

WHAT TO SAY: *You are going to have a lot of fun! I'll be right here if you need me.*

This works whether you are in the next room or just a phone call away. He'll find solace in knowing that you are available in case he needs you.

WHAT NOT TO SAY: *Don't be a chicken.*

VARIATION: *Don't act like a baby.*

Trying something new, especially something that requires stepping outside the comfort zone of family, can be very intimidating and often downright scary. Telling a six-year-old to tough it out for the night isn't the best advice to give as you are pushing him out the door.

What We Have Here Is a Failure to Communicate

There will come a day when your child is noticeably distant, quiet, or distracted. Chances are you will let it pass as something trivial, and it may very well be. However, drastic changes in behavior, especially when an otherwise engaging conversationalist becomes suddenly and awkwardly shy, could mean that your kid is keeping a secret. It is up to you to determine the significance of it and assess whether the subject matter being withheld is something that needs to be discussed openly.

To be clear, there is nothing wrong with children keeping secrets—everybody needs something special that is just their own. However, a child's reluctance to speak about something that is troubling her should be taken very seriously.

TYPICAL PHRASE YOU MAY HEAR: *Nothing. That's the point: You won't be hearing anything from a previously talkative child.*

Again, a child with a secret is not a big deal. Generally speaking, when they have something they want to keep quiet, they are pretty obvious about it, which makes our job so much easier.

TYPICAL PHRASE YOU MAY HEAR: *I know something I can't tell you!*

VARIATION: *I know what we got you for your birthday! I know who the surprise is for!*

Secrets can be exciting. The key is to get an idea of what it may be without actually ruining it.

WHAT TO SAY: *Ohh! Come on, spill it!*

VARIATION: *Don't ruin it!*

Yes, these are opposite in terms of whether to share the secret, but they are on the same level as far as playfulness with the child is concerned. It's all about setting the scene. You can tell a lot about the seriousness of the secret from the child's body language.

Kids are entitled to their secrets as long as they are of a childish nature. Unfortunately, that isn't always the case.

TYPICAL PHRASE YOU MAY HEAR: *I can't talk about it.*

VARIATIONS: *I'm not allowed to say. I'm afraid to tell you.*

If a child has a secret, then chances are she heard it or created it with someone else, and that someone is most likely her friend. If you are concerned about the information being shared and/or withheld, don't be afraid to contact other parents to snoop it out.

However, in a perfect world, your child will be comfortable enough opening up to you should the secret require it.

WHAT TO SAY: *You can tell me anything.*

If the kid doesn't approach you, maybe it's just none of your business. Have you considered that possibility?

WHAT TO SAY: *Did someone do something bad?*

VARIATION: *Did someone do something to you? Did you do something wrong? Did anyone get hurt?*

Try to be serious enough to help the child realize it is important to answer these questions, but try not to show intense emotion at this point. In most cases it is probably nothing, and pushing the subject may be a delicate matter. But in the final analysis, if you fear that your child is keeping something in that needs to be addressed, don't be afraid to track the information down on your own. No secret is as important as the safety and well-being of your child.

Imagine All the Friends

Have you ever heard all about your child's new friend—she goes on and on well beyond the point of comfort and then introduces you . . . to an empty chair?

Meet her imaginary friend, and use your manners.

The world of imaginary friends is a big one. Friends might come in the form of kids, mustached unicorns, talking sandwiches, or giant trees—whatever your child's imagination can produce.

TYPICAL PHRASE YOU MAY HEAR: *This is my friend Mr. Bumblecorn Sycamore. He's a giant tree.*

VARIATION: *This is Bob. He's a BLT.*

Many parents feel the immediate need to scoff at the elephant (or whatever imaginary friend) in the room, invisible though it may be. But take a breath and hold it in. There is no reason to squash imaginative play, and that is exactly what this is. Imaginary friends are a very common part of childhood, and there is no need for alarm.

WHAT TO SAY: *It is a pleasure to meet you. Welcome to our home.*

Humor them. For the most part, kids are very aware that it is all an elaborate charade, and the creation of imaginary friends is just an outlet for them to explore in new and different ways.

WHAT NOT TO SAY: *I don't see a tree.*

VARIATIONS: *Bob isn't kosher.*

You don't have to see to believe.

Granted, some kids take imaginary friends to the extreme and refuse to do anything without their constant companionship, which may lead to some odd looks in the restaurant. However, most kids move on in good time from this type of creativity. Besides, Bob doesn't eat much.

TYPICAL PHRASE YOU MAY HEAR: *Bob is my only friend.*

This might be different. It sounds like there may be other issues involved, from childhood loneliness to a desperate need to confide in someone without actually telling anyone. Proceed with caution.

WHAT TO SAY: *I'll play with you! What can Bob do that I can't?*

VARIATION: *You have lots of other friends, too. Let's invite one over.*

You have either just cured loneliness or opened the door to a deeper conversation. Your next step depends on recognizing which has occurred.

WHAT NOT TO SAY: *Let's have Bob for lunch.*

You don't know where Bob has been.

Achieving BFF Status

It starts with some laughs on the playground, then maybe they share a couple of carrots at snack time, and before you know it your kid has a new friend. When they both discover that they like the same thing—whatever it is—suddenly we are talking best friend territory. Fun just went up a level. Or several.

The bonds of childhood friendship are some of the strongest we ever make, and this is where they start.

TYPICAL PHRASE YOU MAY HEAR: *We are the best friends ever!*

VARIATION: *Nobody is more fun than my best friend.*

Having someone so close that you consider her or him your best friend is a special feeling, and your child should cherish it accordingly. As a parent, you can reinforce this.

WHAT TO SAY: *A good friend is a real treasure.*

VARIATIONS: *You are very lucky to have each other. I bet you have a lot of fun together!*

Welcome the friend into the fold. Let your home be his home. Ideally, his family will offer something similar to your child as well. Including friends in occasional activities that were once family-centric is a fantastic opportunity for kids to develop their friendships while ensuring that your influence remains a big part of the picture.

WHAT NOT TO SAY: *You don't need to spend so much time with your friends.*

VARIATION: *Friends are nice, but family is better.*

"Family first" is a great motto and an even better practice, but that doesn't mean that friends can't be part of the fun.

Friendships and family relationships have a lot of overlap, but neither can replace the other. They are two different bonds, and the fact that family is king doesn't lessen the importance of a solid friendship. Let each enhance the other. The common ground is happiness.

TYPICAL PHRASE YOU MAY HEAR: *I don't want to do anything with you. I want to do stuff with my friend!*

VARIATION: *This is boring. I want to play with my friend.*

This sort of thing, however, won't fly. Nip it quick.

WHAT TO SAY: *You can play with your friend later. Right now we are doing something together.*

VARIATION: *That's great that you want to play with your friend, but saying mean things to our family is not the way to make it happen.*

The thrill of something new, in this case the friend, often outshines the comfort of what we already have, the family. It happens. Ride it out and keep it in perspective.

WHAT NOT TO SAY: *If you act like that, you will never play with your friend again.*

Don't make threats you can't, or shouldn't, keep. The child's words, though painful, reflect excitement about the new friendship. It isn't about you. Usually.

Of course, along with the highs of friendship comes the potential for lows, too, and they tend to get pretty ugly.

TYPICAL PHRASE YOU MAY HEAR: *We aren't friends anymore.*

VARIATION: *I hate him!*

Every situation is going to be different, but they all have a story. Find out what it is, and address the situation accordingly.

WHAT TO SAY: *What happened? Tell me all about it.*

WHAT NOT TO SAY: *Good riddance.*

Some friendships can be salvaged and are the better for it, and others just run their course. Welcome to life, kid.

The Letter of Friendship

"We're not friends anymore," the boy said from deep within the backseat. His father was driving and couldn't find him in the rearview mirror.

"Why?" he asked. "What happened?"

"He won't play with me," replied the boy. "He told me he was my best friend, but that was a lie."

They were driving down a long and winding road. It was a steep fall straight into the father's gut.

"Just because a friend is playing with someone else doesn't mean he isn't your friend, too."

Quiet.

Then, "I told him I didn't want to be his friend."

"What did he say?" his father asked.

"He said that was good. He said that he lied about being my best friend."

"I don't believe that he meant it. People say mean things when their feelings are hurt. It happens all the time."

"He hurt my feelings first," he answered.

"And then you said something mean. Mean words have a way of spreading."

Then their street was there, where it always was. As they turned the corner, the father found his son in the mirror, a reflection leaning against a window. He was looking through the glass.

"May I see that?" the man asked. The boy handed him the note that he had just been writing.

"Why do you want it?" he asked.

"Because I want to share it," his father said.

"Okay," was all the boy replied.

The man held the note and felt something stir in his eyes.

"I am proud of you," he told his son. "And I always will be."

Dear ████,
I did not mean what I said yesterday. You're my best friend and I love playing soccer with you. I want to be friends again.

Love,
Atticus

The Good Life

This chapter has dealt with a lot of worst-case scenarios and the possibility of negative situations in a child's friendships, not because those things are guaranteed to happen, but because they can.

However, most friendships steer childhood far away from such difficulties. The only phrases you will need will be followed by hugs and laughter. That's the good life.

Embrace it.

TYPICAL PHRASE YOU MAY HEAR: *I am having so much fun!*

VARIATIONS: *This is the best time ever! I love playing with my friends!*

Your kid might be playing with her friends, but you made that happen. You gave that happiness a chance to grow. Smile as wide as you can, and let her take all the credit that she so richly deserves.

WHAT TO SAY: *Me, too!*

VARIATION: *I'm glad you are having fun.*

Watching your child run and laugh with her friends through parks, beaches, zoos, and backyards—that is what it is all about. That is why we do the things we do. Don't be afraid to join right in. Running and laughing is good for everybody.

TYPICAL PHRASE YOU MAY HEAR: *Do you want to play with us?*

VARIATIONS: *Chase us! You're it!*

Maybe your back is aching, your legs hurt, and the sun is in your eyes. But don't let excuses keep you a spectator to your child's life. Jump right in and be as much a part of it as you can.

WHAT TO SAY: *Here I come!*

VARIATION: *Let's do it!*

The thing about childhood is that kids believe it to be infinite, even though they know that they have aged since infancy and will continue to do so. They see us and know that we too were once barefoot and running wild without a care in the world. But age for them is always a day away, and that is what makes every moment so special. There is splendor waiting with each new step and laughter hiding in every baited breath. Children refuse to let such things go unacknowledged.

WHAT NOT TO SAY: *This too shall pass.*

VARIATION: *Enjoy it while you can.*

Why do you keep doing that to everyone? Let the kids make the most of what they have. Sure, you are right, everything is fleeting, but nobody wants to talk about it in the middle of the moment. Don't be a buzzkill.

The bonds of friendship may bend, and a few may break, but they are among the strongest and most rewarding experiences

your child will ever know. Joy, confidence, understanding, support, companionship, and laughter—that's what friends are for. Sing it loudly.

CHAPTER 8

Conflict and Bullies: Words Are the New Sticks and Stones

Remember when kids picking on other kids was just good, clean fun (except for the kids being picked on, of course)? The kids doing the picking didn't mean anything by it. They were just fooling around. Rumor was that it built character.

You have probably heard people say things like that, and some follow it with epic monologues on the hypersensitivity of a generation of entitled kids who are hugged too much.

You are not going to hear that here.

Ours is a world in which children are bullied, beaten, and even killed for pursuing an education, following a religion, talking oddly, or dressing in a manner that society deems wrong.

Don't think that these tragedies only happen somewhere else. Wherever you live, this sort of thing has happened to a child, and it will probably happen again. It is painfully ugly, acutely dangerous, and heartbreakingly preventable.

A lot of what kids do, in terms of pushing an agenda of hate, is based on learned behavior, and that starts in the home. It should stop there, too.

This chapter deals with the words and actions of bullies, their victims, and all of the bystanders who could make a difference.

We can *all* make a difference.

Mean Kids

If we all simply accepted that some kids are just mean by nature, this parenting thing would be a whole lot more straightforward, wouldn't it? Writing a kid off as a bad egg would make dealing with the repercussions of his actions so much easier. The world would be black and white, instead of many shades of gray. However, even the most ornery of children has a tender side, often hidden beneath layers of experiences to which we are not privy. In other words, don't be too quick to assume the worst about someone when his worst behavior may be nothing more than his best defense.

TYPICAL PHRASE YOU MAY HEAR: *A kid at school said that I am stupid.*

VARIATIONS: *One of the kids at school always says mean things to everyone. That kid isn't nice to the rest of us.*

This may be cause for concern, or it could be nothing. The situation needs a bit more monitoring, but you should look into it. If your child thinks someone is threatening other children, let the school know. If the kid in question just wants to be left alone, maybe everyone should respect that (although you should alert authorities at the school just in case the "mean kid" is behaving as he does as a consequence of something that needs to be discussed with a professional).

WHAT TO SAY: *Does that kid have any friends that he plays with?*

VARIATION: *If that kid just wants to be left alone, that's okay, but if he's picking on other kids, you need to let a teacher know.*

There are any number of reasons why a child may act "mean" toward his peers, but if one of them is a lack of friends and/or social insecurities, it couldn't hurt for other kids to show him kindness even though they may receive gruffness in return.

WHAT NOT TO SAY: *If he's mean to you, then you should be mean to him.*

Two wrongs don't make a right. The other child could have a very legitimate excuse for his behavior, but this phrase encourages your kid to act mean out of spite. That is not a good precedent to set.

TYPICAL PHRASE YOU MAY HEAR: *Kids think I'm mean because I don't want to play with them.*

VARIATION: *Kids think I am mean just because I am smarter than they are.*

Someone needs to work on his delivery.

As we discussed earlier, there is nothing wrong with a child wanting to play by himself, and being smart is a good thing. However, declaring other children to be less so is no way to make friends.

WHAT TO SAY: *Maybe instead of saying you don't want to play with them, you could just tell them that you want some time to yourself. Make sure they know it isn't something they have done.*

VARIATIONS: *You are very smart, but telling other kids that you are smarter than they are—even if you could prove it—is not a nice thing to do. There is no reason to use your own success to make others feel bad.*

Tact is a good thing.

FOLLOW-UP: *Would you like it if someone spoke like that to you? Do you understand how it could sound mean? Treat others the way you like to be treated, and everyone will see what a nice kid you are.*

Internet Safety

Kids love technology, and technology (specifically those companies that sell technology) loves kids. However, just because a seven-year-old is savvy enough to surf the Internet does not mean she should. There is some crazy stuff online, and contrary to popular belief, most of it does not involve cats.

TYPICAL PHRASE YOU MAY HEAR: *This site on the Internet wants a credit card number.*

VARIATION: *What is my Social Security number?*

Identity theft is real, and you don't have to be an adult to fall victim to it. Don't let kids search the Internet unsupervised.

WHAT TO SAY: *Let me look at the website and see what it is. Then we will discuss whether or not we are paying for something.*

VARIATION: *Your Social Security number does not belong on the Internet.*

Websites that prey on people for personal information don't care whether you are five or fifty. They just want what you aren't selling, and the easier it is to get it, the better.

WHAT NOT TO SAY: *My credit card number is . . .*

VARIATION: *Your Social Security number is . . .*

Granted, most people know better than to give their credit card number to a child without looking at the site themselves, but it happens. Don't let it happen to you.

And thank you for the Social Security number. Your kid is now in debt.

Sadly, identity theft is the best-case scenario when it comes to worst-case scenarios on the Internet. The real danger to children resides in social media, where cyberbullying has taken cruel and insensitive acts to a new level, and in gaming platforms with chat features that allow child predators to do the unthinkable things that earn them the name. It is sad, sick stuff.

TYPICAL PHRASE YOU MAY HEAR: *The kids at school keep posting pictures of me on Facebook and calling me names.*

VARIATION: *Kids are putting pictures of me on Instagram and saying that I'm _____.*

This is a situation that must be corrected, and it is relatively easy to correct, thankfully. First of all, children are not allowed on social media platforms, nor do they have any business on social media platforms. Many of the more popular sites require users to be at least thirteen years old, but even that seems too young considering the content they will gain access to. Do not let your child use them.

As for the offending party: Take screenshots of all activity, report them to the site, and have the account removed if possible. Contact the school with all the evidence you have gathered, and speak to the offending child's parents. Expect resistance from someone along the way, but don't let that keep you from protecting your child. If the situation is serious enough, go public with the information. It could get ugly, but not nearly as ugly as what can happen if you don't act.

WHAT NOT TO SAY: *They are just teasing you.*

Don't take your child's pain lightly. When left unchecked, these things have a way of snowballing.

TYPICAL PHRASE YOU MAY HEAR: *My friend from the game wants to meet me after school. She said I shouldn't tell anyone.*

VARIATION: *Someone in the game chat wants to visit me at home. I gave them our address.*

This is the scariest of all Internet scenarios. As any parent will surely attest, the idea of a predator targeting your child is beyond frightening.

The fact that your child tells you anything at all about this is something of a victory. This is why it is so important to have open lines of communication in your family, as well as a clear understanding of what information is—and what information isn't—appropriate to reveal to strangers and "friends" on the Internet.

It is possible that the person in question really is another child and that it is all innocent banter, but be sure to follow up with the site and the authorities to get a clear answer. It is better to overreact than not to react at all.

WHAT TO SAY: *I am so glad you came to me with this information. Let's look into it and see what we need to do.*

VARIATION: *You did the right thing by coming to me. Good job.*

This is where you take the steps outlined earlier and make sure that your child is safe and protected.

WHAT NOT TO SAY: *This is your fault.*

VARIATION: *I told you this would happen.*

Do not blame the child. If you want to blame anyone, blame yourself for not paying more attention to her online activity.

The possibilities outlined earlier are not presented to cause you needless worry, but rather to ensure your awareness of very real dangers and explain how to react to them. Most children will never face these situations, but you should take the proper steps to prevent them all the same.

Technology is many things, but it is not a babysitter.

JOIN THE CLUB

There are some fantastic gaming platforms online, such as Disney's Club Penguin, that make safe chat possible for kids. These games have their own highly sophisticated, proprietary systems in place to allow children creative expression through chat without sharing personal information or engaging in activity that could lead to bullying. However, the best thing a parent can do is to be involved. Play with your children, or be in the immediate vicinity, whenever they go online.

Beyond Cooties

We discussed "cooties" in an earlier chapter. Although verbal abuse certainly qualifies as bullying, it generally stops short of physical altercation. Not all bullying is so restrained.

There is a long list of reasons why one child might bully another, and none of it holds even the thinnest shred of legitimacy. There is no "reason" to justify a child being victimized by another—ever.

From the classic threats to exact milk money, through giving wedgies in the hallway, to intense verbal and physical violence, our children walk through a minefield of potential abuse at the hands of their peers. Their best defense is to tell someone about it.

TYPICAL PHRASE YOU MAY HEAR: *If I don't give them my lunch money, they are going to beat me up.*

VARIATION: *They said I am too fat and ugly to live.*

Kids are capable of saying terrible things. Often they do not comprehend the vitriol behind such statements, because they have put little to no thought into the words. And many have never been victimized by such cruelty themselves, so they lack any perspective that could lead to empathy. That doesn't mean the words don't hurt.

Such verbal taunts, of course, represent the "best-case" scenario where bullying is concerned. When there is actual malice behind the message, and intent to frighten or do harm, that is a criminal act and should be reported to the proper authorities.

WHAT TO SAY: *We will talk to their parents/teacher/ counselor immediately.*

Then do it.

When the child is being attacked with words of hate and/or violence, you should contact the appropriate authorities, up to and including the police. You may also want to consider seeking professional help for your child. More than anything, make sure he knows that the bully is very, very wrong.

WHAT TO SAY: *You are beautiful, and I love you more than anything in the world.*

VARIATION: *Anything with love as the message, said loudly and often.*

Make sure your child understands, acknowledges, and accepts that the bully is wrong. Show him that he is greatly loved, and hug him as long as he will let you. Then hug him again.

WHAT NOT TO SAY: *They're just messing with you.*

VARIATION: *Try to stay away from them.*

Although neither phrase is incorrect, both suggest that you are not taking the matter seriously. *Do not take bullying lightly.* Whether those antagonizing your child mean him actual harm or not, your child believes they do, and this demands nothing less than your full attention. Children can be very sensitive to criticism from other kids, especially if it is someone they look up to. Do *not* let this escalate.

Talk to your kid.

When Your Kid Is the Bully

Nobody wants their kid to be the victim of a bully, so we tend to take an active role in preventing such situations from escalating. But what happens when the bully *is* your child?

TYPICAL PHRASE YOU MAY HEAR: *Ha! Those kids are all scared of me.*

VARIATIONS: *I don't let the other kids get away with stuff. I am the boss of the playground.*

Granted, these phrases alone do not a bully make, but chances are that if your child is threatening, frightening, or hurting other kids, you will hear about it.

WHAT TO SAY: *Why would you want kids to be scared of you? That is not a good way to make friends.*

VARIATIONS: *It isn't your job to keep the other kids in line. Nobody made you the boss of anyone.*

The sooner you are able to approach your child about his negative behavior, the better it will be for everyone involved. It is much easier to apologize for hurt feelings than for broken bones.

The key is empathy and conversation.

Start by accepting such a thing as even possible. Our child? A bully? He wouldn't hurt a fly! Well, maybe.

WHAT NOT TO SAY: *I bet they are scared of you. You're a tough one.*

VARIATIONS: *Somebody has to keep the other kids in line. Does the boss of the playground get his own bathroom?*

The minute your suspicions are confirmed, it is time to go into full crisis mode. That doesn't mean you drink three pots of coffee and run around screaming. Rather, you speak with your child, assess the situation, and get professional help if needed—all while making sure that the victims of your child's words and actions are also cared for and that their needs are met.

Let your child see this. He needs to know what consequences his negative behavior has had for the people he loves. There are victims on both sides of the bully.

TYPICAL PHRASE YOU MAY HEAR: *I was just messing with them.*

VARIATIONS: *It was a joke. I was trying to be funny.*

They say some people can't take a joke, but what you never hear about are those who can't tell one.

Tell your kid not to quit the day job, and then take that sincerity on tour—there are amends to be made.

WHAT TO SAY: *Do you understand why the other kids are upset?*

VARIATION: *Put yourself in their shoes, and see how funny you think it is.*

Don't be afraid to play a bit of hardball here, even if he seems to be coming around. He needs to understand that bullying behavior is not tolerated and that his attempt at humor missed the mark.

WHAT NOT TO SAY: *Some people just like to whine.*

VARIATION: *Those kids are too sensitive.*

There is a difference between hypersensitivity and genuine distress. It isn't hard to find.

Sticking Up for Others

It takes a special person to stick up for someone else, especially when doing so may result in negative consequences. Therefore, it becomes a dangerous thing to encourage in children. On the other hand, if you want your kids to do the right thing, you can't teach them to go halfway. The principle to communicate—by instruction and example—is that if someone is being wronged, you should do your best to stop it—or get hold of someone who can. Your kids will be better people for it.

TYPICAL PHRASE YOU MAY HEAR: *They couldn't defend themselves, so I did.*

VARIATION: *They were being picked on, so I told the bully to stop.*

The downside here is that by taking a stand, your child may wind up getting in trouble. By the time an adult is in the mix, your child's involvement may send her straight to the principal's office.

Not only that, but defending someone else is sometimes thankless, and it often results in the defender suffering the same fate as the person he or she is trying to protect—maybe worse. So it's important to reinforce the positive side of your child's behavior.

WHAT TO SAY: *You did the right thing.*

VARIATION: *I am proud of you.*

To be clear, this is not a call to arms. Children should not seek out confrontation, but that does not mean it won't find them, or someone in the general area. To stand by and do nothing when someone is being picked on is the same thing as condoning the action; however, that doesn't mean the child has to be a hero and offer herself as a human shield. Running for help is an honorable course of action, too.

WHAT NOT TO SAY: *You should mind your own business.*

VARIATION: *It's not your problem.*

When a child is picked on, it's everybody's business. Ignoring a bully who harasses kid after kid only allows the problem to get bigger and bigger.

Fun fact about bullies: According to widely circulated playground lore and stereotypes, they tend to back down when someone stands up to them. Multiply that by many "someones," and a once-terrifying menace to playground society may soon find himself looking for a new gig.

WHAT TO SAY: *If you see someone being bullied and there isn't time to get an adult, stand up to them with all of the other kids.*

VARIATION: *There is safety in numbers.*

If escape is an option, take it, but not if that means leaving another child to his or her doom (or whatever the bully is planning). Many kids facing down the one bully is a great way to make bullies rethink the situation.

TYPICAL PHRASE YOU MAY HEAR: *We are all standing up for each other whenever the bully starts being mean.*

VARIATION: *We protect each other.*

That's great, but a call to the school is still in order. The more the group does its thing, the more likely it is that the bully will find ways to confront each of them individually, and you know how that ends.

Pushing, Biting, and Fisticuffs

They say that words can't hurt you, but most people would beg to differ. It never feels good when someone says mean things to or about you. Kids don't have your years of experience and your thick skin from a lifetime of harsh talk to give them perspective. They hear mean words and react. Sometimes there is biting.

TYPICAL PHRASE YOU MAY HEAR: *He kept calling me names, so I bit him.*

VARIATION: *She was biting me, so I pushed her down.*

There are no winners here. Sure, we don't want our children to let others walk all over them, but they need to have enough restraint to refrain from biting. That should never be an option.

That said, you can safely tell your child that if someone is biting him, shove fast and hard if that is the only way to make the other kid stop. Getting bitten hurts!

Children should never look to violence to work through a problem, but when violence is used against them, they have every right to protect themselves.

WHAT TO SAY: *Don't ever bite someone unless your life depends on it. Being called a mean name, regardless of how it felt, does not warrant your use of violence.*

VARIATION: *You did what was necessary to protect yourself after you were bitten, and that should be the extent of using force.*

Some people disagree with this. They think that the proverbial eye for an eye is the way to handle violence, and yes, it is tempting. However, doesn't that mean that *everyone* has sunk to the lowest level? Nobody ever said the high road was easy.

WHAT NOT TO SAY: *You should have punched him in the face.*

VARIATION: *If someone tries to hurt you, you ought to beat the snot out of him.*

Striking out in self-defense, like most things that are exceptions to a rule, may have repercussions in addition to scratches and bruises. If and when your child decides to fight back against an aggressor, he should understand exactly what he's fighting for and be prepared for the consequences that follow such an action.

In the event of an actual fight, where two or more parties start throwing haymakers, jabs, and assorted sucker punches, things get a little gray. Did one attack the other? Or did they agree to meet at high noon and duke it out? In any case, you should discourage fighting as a solution to anything.

TYPICAL PHRASE YOU MAY HEAR: *I got in trouble at school for fighting.*

Any number of questions may run through a parent's mind at this type of news. What does the other person look like? Did your kid win? You may have several other inquiries about the cause and outcome. However, this isn't an MMA cage fight; this is your kid. Chances are, you don't want her or him fighting again.

WHAT TO SAY: *Was it worth it?*

Only they know the answer to that one. Chances are they will say no and you can discuss the lessons learned. Then again, they may say, "Yes, totally!" and who knows? Maybe it was. There are lessons to be learned there, too.

CHAPTER 9

Winning and Losing: How They Play the Game

Winning isn't everything. We know that, but the truth is that winning is pretty awesome. In fact, given a choice, most people actually prefer winning to not winning. However, that does not mean that losing is without merit. There is something to be said for playing the game to the best of your ability, outcome be damned.

Society likes to suggest otherwise. Television, movies, and the Internet constantly bombard us with one clear message: You are either a winner or a loser. There is little room for middle ground.

Kids are not immune to this barrage. Have you ever been to a youth baseball game or soccer match? It seems that there's always at least one parent yelling at umpires, coaches, other parents, and (worse) the kids, with language best saved for the major leagues. These people take winning pretty seriously, and your kid better not mess it up.

Every other person within earshot thinks it is a fairly sad and embarrassing way to act, but that won't keep certain parents from doing it. *Their* kid has to be a winner.

The pressure to win is great, and it presents problems. After all, it is admirable to strive for success, but flaunting success at the expense of others is not something to be proud of. There is no shame in winning, but there is no shame in losing, either. The only shameful behavior in this scenario is standing in the crowd and acting like a jackass. Remember, it *is* just a game.

This chapter is about winning, losing, and all that really matters.

Good Sport, Bad Sport

The only thing worse than watching someone throw a public fit over losing a competitive event is watching even louder, even more obnoxious behavior on the part of the person who won. Sore losers are ugly to watch, but a bad winner is an assault on the senses.

Need an example? Head down to the park and watch a child's soccer match or baseball game. You'll see tasteless, self-congratulatory behavior on the field, and sometimes it spills over to the parents sitting next to you. Somehow, everyone is embarrassed but them.

TYPICAL PHRASE YOU MAY HEAR: *We won! We won!*

This is great. This is celebrating a battle hard fought. There is nothing wrong with showing emotion and excitement when you win.

WHAT TO SAY: *Congratulations. You played a great game. Now let's shake hands with the other team. They tried hard, too!*

Sportsmanship is the key to competition. The other team is an opponent, not the enemy. Shake their hands, win or lose.

TYPICAL PHRASE YOU MAY HEAR: *We beat them! They are losers!*

VARIATIONS: *You suck! In your face! We kicked your butt!*

Chances are the other team is fully aware that they lost, and it is a safe bet that they don't like it. Rubbing their face in it serves no purpose but to compound negative feelings and to show disrespect for the game, the opposing players, and their effort.

WHAT TO SAY: *When you make fun of the competition, you are really criticizing your own efforts.*

VARIATIONS: *You will lose games, too. Do you want other teams to treat you like that?*

Again, there is nothing wrong with enjoying the moment. Your kid just achieved her goal, and she played hard. Enjoy it. Just encourage her to be nice about it.

TYPICAL PHRASE YOU MAY HEAR: *They played a great game. They are a very good team.*

VARIATIONS: *It was awesome to play against them. They were tough.*

There is grace in crediting the competition after the game, whether your child's team won or lost. She couldn't have done either without the competition, and she should be aware of that. Her team didn't succeed in a vacuum; they beat a team that worked just as hard as they did.

WHAT TO SAY: *It isn't whether you win or lose, but how you play the game.*

Yes, it is one of the oldest clichés in the book, but it is true. It means that winning by playing dirty or bending the rules of the competition to gain an advantage over the opponent is incredibly dishonest and lacking in good sportsmanship.

WHAT NOT TO SAY: *You get out there and win, no matter what.*

Winning by any means necessary isn't always winning. Winning is playing your hardest and having fun while doing it.

Cheer as loud as you can for your player, regardless of the outcome.

The Success of Failure

There is a reason why the old adage "If at first you don't succeed, try and try again" has remained in our vernacular, and it isn't just because practice makes perfect. It is because nothing teaches better than failure. The more we try, the more we fail, then the better our chances of eventual success.

TYPICAL PHRASE YOU MAY HEAR: *We lost.*

VARIATIONS: *We didn't win and I don't want to play anymore.*

Losing may sting, but it also offers the child an opportunity to reflect on what he did right and what he could have done better. Kids should take advantage of the lesson and apply it to their preparation for the next game.

Sometimes that sting is more than they care to bear, and they would rather not play at all. Don't let them go out on a bitter note of disappointment.

WHAT TO SAY: *You played hard, but there is always room for improvement. What do you think we should work on?*

VARIATION: *Don't ever give up.*

If your child wants to stop participating in a sport, then make sure the feeling is based on the big picture and not a knee-jerk reaction to losing a competition. That said, if he's made a commitment to a team, he needs to honor it. He can re-evaluate his plans for next year in the off-season. Being part of a team means being there for your teammates, win or lose. That in itself can be a tough lesson to learn. Nobody has ever won by not playing.

WHAT NOT TO SAY: *You made a lot of mistakes.*

VARIATIONS: *You aren't very good. Maybe you should quit.*

Make sure that children who accept their losses as a learning opportunity are not accepting losing as a culture. Even though winning isn't everything, nobody wants to compete against someone who doesn't care. That makes for a hollow victory. The thrill of competition derives from playing against those who have prepared themselves to do their very best.

TYPICAL PHRASE YOU MAY HEAR: *I know what I did wrong, and I know what I need to do to fix it.*

VARIATION: *I could have done some things differently.*

Your kid is accepting that he's getting better with every game, practice, and experience. He's learning that a lack of success on the field can inspire future success by promoting understanding of what went wrong and how to fix it. The ability to learn from our own mistakes and work toward correcting them is something that will benefit children throughout their lives.

It is good to get better.

The Game of Life

One of the best side effects of sport is the health and exercise awareness that children gain from their activities. So keep in mind that in addition to everything we've said about team play, confidence, and social interaction, there is yet one more positive: The kids are getting fit.

Most sports require a fair amount of running, jumping, throwing, and catching. These improve coordination, strength, stamina, and the child's overall health. Plus, it is a lot of fun. It is a pretty nice positive.

TYPICAL PHRASE YOU MAY HEAR: *Will you go running with me? I need to stay in shape for soccer.*

VARIATION: *Will you do some jumping jacks with me? I want to get stronger.*

And just like that, your kid became your personal trainer. It's a win–win.

WHAT TO SAY: *Of course. Let me change my shoes.*

VARIATION: *I need to stay in shape, too!*

Being fit and active is something that will benefit children (and their parents) in many ways throughout their lives. It is a wonderful routine to establish—and a fantastic lifestyle to share as a family.

WHAT NOT TO SAY: *No, go play outside.*

VARIATIONS: *I don't have time for that. You ran enough at school.*

Chances are you need the exercise as much as your child does (and probably quite a bit more). These phrases not only discourage your kid from being active but also set an example of apathy in regard to fitness and health. That is not a good mindset to fall into at any age.

Be active, and encourage your child to do the same.

TYPICAL PHRASE YOU MAY HEAR: *I don't like playing sports. I just want to ride my bike.*

It's like they have no idea.

Children do not have to be involved in organized sports in order to maintain a fit and healthy lifestyle. If they don't like kickball, take them hiking, surfing, jogging, biking, or skating, or just play long games of tag across the entire park—anything that gets them up and moving. Everyone will be better for it.

TYPICAL PHRASE YOU MAY HEAR: *People who are healthy usually live longer. You should exercise more.*

Your kid has been paying attention, and she is worried about you.

Talk to your children about fitness and exercise, and find ways to take part in them together. Set goals and strive to meet them. That is quality time at its finest.

WHAT TO SAY: *Last one to the slide is a rotten egg!*

Then run, run, and run some more. Laugh loudly to really sell it.

Last of the Rotten Eggs

For some children, the idea of losing is almost too much to bear. The competitive culture of school, play, and life is overwhelming, and frankly, they aren't very good at competing and/or just don't enjoy it.

It gets pretty old.

TYPICAL PHRASE YOU MAY HEAR: *I always lose at everything.*

VARIATION: *The other kids are right. I am a loser.*

No child should feel like that.

Although much can be said about the benefits of healthy competition, the simple fact is that some children do not respond to it in the manner in which kids who enjoy it do. Unfortunately, those kids tend to be overlooked by the system and spend their youth dreading organized activities and resenting those who are involved in them.

That isn't good for anyone.

WHAT TO SAY: *You are not a loser.*

VARIATION: *How you place in a game does not reflect how you place in life.*

The thing about games is that they are just games. However, our society treats sporting events and professional athletes as though they carry the weight of the world upon their broad, wealthy shoulders. That mentality trickles down from professional to college and other amateur athletes, until it lands somewhere on the playground and a kid picks it up. You know the rest.

WHAT NOT TO SAY: *You need to try harder to be a winner.*

VARIATION: *It embarrasses me that you don't try harder.*

First, this isn't about you. Second, that's just mean.

Everyone loves to excel, and parents enjoy watching their children do well, yet we often put too much pressure on children for results that they cannot, or will not, produce. Instead of making them feel worse about it, why not find other avenues and passions to explore?

It's just a game.

WHAT NOT TO SAY: *If you don't play the game, other people are going to make fun of you.*

At the end of the day, it doesn't matter what other people think. The only thing that matters is that your child is safe and happy. She does not need to define herself in terms of the labels all around us. And she most certainly is not a loser, no matter how many games she doesn't win.

WHAT TO SAY: *What would you like to do?*

VARIATION: *This is your story. Don't let other people tell it.*

Children should never have to worry about being good enough.

The Picking Order

Few things in childhood sting like the social stigma of being picked last. It is a public shaming for not being quite as fast, strong, or tall as the next kid. For the most part, there is nothing the child can do but stand there and take it.

Frankly, it is embarrassing.

In theory, this could inspire the child to work harder and try to improve his aptitude for whatever the game may be, but what if he doesn't like or care about the game? It seems kind of silly to waste time on something that he's only participating in because the P.E. teacher insists on it.

TYPICAL PHRASE YOU MAY HEAR: *I was picked last for kickball.*

VARIATION: *Nobody ever picks me.*

See? It stings.

There are a few different approaches that we as parents can take. Do we want to help change the status quo, or do we want to make it easier for the child to live with the situation? That part is up to him.

WHAT TO SAY: *Do you like kickball?*

VARIATION: *Do you want to be picked sooner?*

If he does like kickball (make sure he doesn't say no just because he was picked last), and assuming he wants to be picked sooner, then go outside and start playing it. Play it all the time. He'll have fun and he'll get better. Plus, it is quality time together.

Your kid might get picked last a few more times, but once the other children notice the improvement, your child will move up the picking order as his skill set dictates.

If he doesn't like kickball, you might want to play it anyway. Kickball is fun, and maybe playing with you will change his mind about the game.

WHAT NOT TO SAY: *They are just picking the popular kids first.*

VARIATION: *It sounds like a popularity contest.*

You are trying to help, but not only did you just confirm that your child isn't good at the game in question, but you also implied that he isn't popular with his peers. That's a double whammy.

There really is only one surefire way to improve his chances of being picked sooner, and that is embracing the game and getting better at it.

Anything short of courting improvement is accepting the situation and moving on. Not that there is anything wrong with that. Somebody has to be picked last, and we are all picked last for something.

WHAT TO SAY: *I'll pick you first. Every single time.*

RUNNING ON THE FAST TRACK

The trouble with singling young children out as good or bad at certain sports is that they might actually believe it. Kids who show an aptitude for athletics based on nothing more than an early growth spurt tend to get funneled into a system that works harder with them to develop whatever skills they may have. Late bloomers subsequently get less opportunity to improve theirs. The former are captains and starters; the latter sit on the bench watching grass grow.

It would be interesting to see how teams would fill out if all kids received equal attention and equivalent opportunities for development throughout their growth cycle.

We're All Winners

At the end of the day, it doesn't matter how we are placed or ranked by anyone. It doesn't matter if we have a case full of trophies, a rainbow of medals, or letters sewn across our jacket. All that matters is that we gave our best at everything we tried, and we had as much fun as humanly possible.

We are all examples, and there is not an off switch.

TYPICAL PHRASE YOU MAY HEAR: *You are my hero.*

VARIATION: *You are my role model.*

That is a lot of responsibility, and with it comes great power. Make the most of it.

WHAT TO SAY: *That makes me feel very special. I'll try to be worthy of the honor.*

If you take just one thing from this book, here it is: The secret to successful parenting isn't money, status, or any other classification that society throws your way. It doesn't matter whether you are a two-parent family, single, gay, straight, adoptive, foster, or other. All that matters is that you are full of love and respect, and you do your best to share it with those who count on you.

Children who grow up loved are already winners, and anything else is just icing on the cake.

TYPICAL PHRASE YOU MAY HEAR: *My favorite thing to do is spend time with you.*

It is so hard to give kids the attention they deserve, and to be fair, they need their own space just as much as we do, but that doesn't mean we should spend our time passing each other in the hall with nods and silence like so many coworkers. Our job as parents is to be involved.

WHAT TO SAY: *That is my favorite thing, too.*

VARIATION: *I always look forward to spending time with you.*

There is a school of thought that maintains that we shouldn't be "soft" on our kids—that by giving them affection rather than hard knocks, we are doing them a terrible disservice by not preparing them for life.

That simply isn't true.

The hard knocks of life will work their way into the picture on their own schedule. There is no reason to invite them in early.

WHAT NOT TO SAY: *We spend too much time together.*

VARIATIONS: *We don't hug. We shake hands. There is no reason to get emotional.*

There is every reason to get emotional. Life is short, hard, and sweet. We are lucky enough to have some time to share it with those whom we love and to guide each other through the twists and turns that rise to greet us.

Children are not just giant sponges, soaking up the world. They also pass on, to any of us willing to listen, the knowledge they acquire on their journey.

Be willing to listen.

Children are amazing, and nothing is ever going to change that. Appreciate everything.

TYPICAL PHRASE YOU MAY HEAR: *I love you.*

WHAT TO SAY: *I love you, too.*

Conclusion

People like to say that there are no right or wrong answers. Although that may hold true in a lot of cases, there are exceptions. Parenting is one of them. There are definitely things parents can do and say that are right and others that are absolutely wrong.

We have all made parenting mistakes, and chances are we will continue to do so. Luckily, mistakes are also the best tools for teaching, and the ability to learn from our own experiences is what makes good parents great (according to assorted coffee mugs and various school projects).

Kids make mistakes, too. In fact, making mistakes is par for the childhood course. There are times when our bad response may compound the damage. It happens. Keep it in perspective, learn from it, apologize when needed, and move on. Dwelling on failures is the surest way to avoid success.

What we do today is the foundation for what our children will do tomorrow. Yes, it is a lot of pressure, but that doesn't mean it shouldn't also be fun. After all, is there anything better than the sound of a child's laughter?

To that end, the way we act *in front of* our children is just as important as how we act *with* our children. We are never off the example stage, and it is how we act when we don't know the kids are watching that will resonate with them in the years to come. We want them to be the best people they can be. Possible side effects include bettering ourselves in the process. That's a win–win.

What is important is that we keep an open mind, pay attention, and listen. Listening is key, as are always being there for our kids, hearing what they say, and looking beyond it for the full meaning of their words. That is where we will find true understanding.

Even with all the joy, it is still a melancholy journey in places, full of mishaps and milestones. Some experiences may resonate more than others, but none should be taken for granted. You may not get a second chance.

Above all, don't let your concerns for the future keep you from enjoying the now. Today is when the good stuff happens, and today will be tomorrow before you know it. And so forth and so on.

Consider this: The enjoyment of childhood isn't just for the kids. Most parents will tell you that having children is the greatest experience they have ever known, but sadly, it is short and fleeting. Make the most of the time you have.

No pressure at all.

Index

About the Author

Whit Honea is an award-winning writer and blogger. His essays on parenting and childhood have been published on Babble, BabyCenter, Parentables, The Stir, Good Men Project, Huffington Post, DadCentric, GeekDad, Yahoo!, and numerous other sites. His personal blog, *Honea Express* ("Honea" sounds like "pony"), has been listed as a top parenting blog by many publications over the years, and it has appeared in the *New York Times* and in *Details* and *Parenting* magazines. If you have seen him on TV, you have his deepest sympathies.

He was nominated for a Pushcart Prize for his fiction, and his short stories and poetry have appeared in several anthologies and collections.

Whit currently lives in the Los Angeles area with his wife, two boys, and two dogs. They (the family, not the dogs) divide their time among the beach, museums, and Disneyland. Nobody knows what the dogs do with their downtime.

Visit Whit on Twitter (@whithonea) and his personal website Honea Express at *www.whithonea.com*.